A 31-Day Journey
to Personal Revival

Thirsty

JAMIE MORGAN

PrayerShop
Publishing

Terre Haute, Indiana

PrayerShop Publishing is the publishing arm of the Church Prayer Leaders Network. The Church Prayer Leaders Network exists to equip and inspire local churches and their prayer leaders in their desire to disciple their people in prayer and to become a "house of prayer for all nations." Its online store, prayershop.org, has more than 150 prayer resources available for purchase or download.

ISBN (Print): 978-1-970176-11-7
ISBN (E-Book): 978-1-970176-12-4

1 2 3 4 5 | 2025 2024 2023 2022 2021

Dedication

Lord Jesus, I dedicate this book to *You.*
I pray all who hold this book in their hands will
encounter You with Your revival fire.
Use them as fire starters to set the world
ablaze with the gospel of Jesus Christ.
I love You, Lord!

Acknowledgments

Without certain people, this book wouldn't have been written. I cherish what they've contributed to its pages. It's with the deepest gratitude that I acknowledge the following people for their help with this, my fourth book:

To my faithful husband, Kurt –
I simply couldn't do the work of ministry without you! Faithful is your middle name. You've been by my side every step of the way. Saying thank you doesn't seem enough for all you've done! Love you, Kurt!

To my wonderful son, Shane –
You're the best son in the entire world and remain the shining achievement of my life. I'm blessed beyond measure to be your mother. It astounds me that God chose me to be your mom. He gave me the best when He gave me you. I'm godly proud of the man you've become. I love you more than words can say!

To my sweet daughter-in-law, Ashley –
You're the best wife and mother to my son and granddaughters that I could ever hope for! You are, without a doubt, an answer to this mother's prayers! Love you, Ash!

To my beautiful granddaughters, Claire Abigail and Hannah Jane –
As I write this, you are five and three. My prayer is that you'll carry the torch of my faith in Jesus to the next generation, however and wherever He leads. You, Claire and Hannah, are my sweet reward, my bright spot, my delight, and my human inspiration for everything I do—including writing this book. I love you more than words can say!

To my amazing mother, Dorothy Pancoast –
You and Dad raised me to be a leader. Every person I reach in ministry is the fruit of your labor—including this book! You were also my very first ministry partner. Thank you for everything you have done for me. I love you, Mommy!

To my dear friend, JoAnn Kates –
Years before anyone saw the call of God on my life, you did. You've taken God's mandate to pray for me every day of your life with extreme gravity. For that, I'm eternally grateful. Thank you for all you do to help me accomplish God's call on my life. I love and appreciate you, Joey, more than you'll ever know!

To my awesome Life Church family –
You have traveled this journey with me. You have prayed for me, loved me, supported me, and cheered me on! Pastoring Life Church is one of the greatest joys of my life! Thank you for being the best church in the world! I love you all!

To the anointed Noon Hour Prayer Intercessors –
You've upheld me and this book in prayer. As a result, you share in every blessing and reward. Only heaven records the results of your daily work of prayer. Many are your rewards! I'm so very grateful for each and every one of you and love you dearly!

And lastly, to PrayerShop Publishing and publisher, Jonathan Graf –
Thank you for investing in this book and in me. It was a true honor to work with the publishing arm of America's National Prayer Committee, of which I'm honored to be a member. Thank you for all you do for the Lord and His Church. You're deeply appreciated!

Table of Contents

Directions for Your Journey

Every journey has a destination, and this journey is no exception. Your goal for the next 31 days: *personal revival*.

Thirsty is an interactive devotional that focuses on 31 vital aspects of your Christian walk. Each day you'll embrace the fire of revival for one specific area of your relationship with God and invite Him to bring that area back to life. As you draw near to God every day during this 31-day journey, the All-Consuming Fire will draw near to you, setting your heart on fire for Him.

View yourself at the bottom of a mountain. (That's not hard for me to imagine. I'm writing this at the base of the Rocky Mountains.) One step at a time, you'll climb higher and higher toward your goal of personal revival. But here is a warning: this journey will require *sacrifice*. Determine now you'll not stop. If you completely give yourself to this life-changing journey, it could very well be the best month of your relationship with God.

Here are some tips to make the most of your journey to personal revival:

- **Give yourself to the process**. I mean *really* give yourself to it. On day one, anoint yourself with oil (from your kitchen cabinet) to consecrate yourself to God. Tell Him your heart's desire is to burn for Him. Invite the Holy Spirit to move in your life. Guard and protect the time you have dedicated to this study—as if your life depends upon it.

- **Add fasting to your journey.** We fast to humble ourselves before God. Fasting, coupled with prayer, will prepare the fireplace of your heart for the fire God wants to light. It'll also cause you to hunger after Him more fully. Ask God what type of fast He would have you undertake during all or part of this journey.

- **Honesty and transparency are required.** In order to derive the most from this journey, get gut-level honest about matters of your heart. Don't hold back. To assist you, I've endeavored to be as transparent as possible regarding my own life. Be real with God about your struggles, hurts, and disappointments. This is a safe place to do the hard things.

- **Lay your heart on God's altar.** Your *whole* heart. Every day, lay bare your heart before God. Allow Him to search your heart with His Holy Spirit flashlight. Ask Him to deal with places in your heart that perhaps have cobwebs. God wants to soften, heal, take out, put in, rearrange, and set free so He can—*BOOM*—set your heart ablaze for Him. Revival happens first in the heart.

- **Bring your Bible and journal to each session.** Read, reflect, and meditate on the Scripture passage for each day. Allow the Holy Spirit to give you needed revelation to apply to your life. And then record in your journal, day-by-day, God's transforming work. For years to come, you'll be able to look back on this 31-day season and see the hand of God at work in your life.

- **Take the time to reflect.** The "Questions for Reflection" are for individual use as well as for group discussion. They'll help you hit pause and think about what you just read. Please don't skip this crucial step. Reflecting on what God has spoken to you will turn head knowledge into deep heart revelation.

- **Review is built in.** Every day you'll "Look Back" at what God accomplished in your heart the day before. Although each day focuses on a different aspect of your Christian walk, biblical concepts are periodically repeated throughout—on purpose. This will dig your spiritual well deeper and give you greater capacity to receive, believe, and pour out. Avoid the "I know that already" mindset. I don't and neither do you. We can't hear it enough.

- **Invite others to join you.** Build accountability into this process by asking others to take the journey with you. Offer this study to a friend, a small group, your church, or even on social media as a book study. Challenge, pray for, and encourage one another on your quest for personal revival.

- **Share your personal revival testimony.** After completing this journey, inform your friends and family about the impact *Thirsty* made on your Christian walk. This will encourage them to take their own 31-day journey. Post a selfie on social media holding this book with *#Thirsty31Journey.*

Commitment to Personal Revival

There's something about committing yourself up front. If you do, you'll give yourself fully to it. Decide right now that you're committed to see this 31-day journey to completion. Also, ask your pastor or a trusted Christian friend to pray for you before you begin.

I dedicate myself for the next 31 days to thirst after Jesus like never before. Each and every day I will embrace the fire of God in one specific area of my Christian walk and ask God to bring that area back to life. I won't allow myself to get distracted or deterred. I'll take this journey of personal revival as seriously as I should. I give God full access to my heart and life and give Him permission to do whatever He needs to do. And I'll enjoy every single moment of this life-transforming process of personal revival.

_____   _____

Your Signature   **Date**

Fasten your seatbelt.
You're in for the ride of your life!

Psalm 63:1

O God, you are my God;

I earnestly search for you.

My soul thirsts for you;

my whole body longs for you

in this parched and weary land

where there is no water.

DAY 1

Thirsty for Personal Revival

JOHN 1:19–34

You're thirsty **for personal revival.**

How do I know? You wouldn't be holding this book in your hand otherwise. You want true biblical Christianity. The kind you read about in the New Testament. Lukewarm, cultural, go-with-the-flow, worldly Christianity (as if there were such things) will never do.

You want to radically burn and shine like John the Baptist (minus the locusts and camel hair). Jesus described John the Baptist as the greatest man who had ever lived. He lived…and died…to point the way to Jesus.

I want to burn and shine for Jesus like that. I want to prepare the way for the second coming of the Lord. I know you do as well.

John the Baptist's ministry was forged in the desert. Howling winds, endless ribbons of sand, and no relief. The desert produces thirst. Thirst leads to seeking water. Seeking water brings about finding water. Finding water leads to drinking to your fill. Drinking to your fill imparts abundant life.

You don't have to wait for the apathetic, lukewarm Church to get revived in order to experience personal revival. You can get on fire for God now. You can be a living, breathing, walking revival—setting everything you touch ablaze for God!

But personal revival starts with thirst. God uses the desert to create an unquenchable thirst for Jesus. Nothing this world offers will satisfy. Nothing. Only Jesus.

It's in the crucible of the desert that God brings you to a point of insatiable thirst and holy desperation for Him. It's here He shows you there is more—much, much more—than what you're living.

Many view the believers' faith in the four Gospels and Book of Acts as living, impossible-to-attain, super-saint Christianity. But for thirsty Christians, this radical level of faith is both achievable by the grace of God—and the goal. Thirsty Christians don't measure their walks with God by the Christians around them, or even by someone who's done great exploits for God. Jesus is now the standard.

A Christian who has been personally revived lives true biblical Christianity. Not perfect Christianity. If that were the case, none of us could experience personal revival. I certainly couldn't. I need God's mercy almost daily. I know I'm not alone.

The road to true biblical Christianity isn't easy. Going against the tide is beyond difficult. Persecution can be deadly. Standing firm to the end is what few will do. Life on the rocky Narrow Road is lonely; most take up residence on the sandy Wide Road. No, true biblical Christianity isn't easy, but is made possible by Jesus' death, burial, resurrection, and ascension.

It's important to note that John never left the desert. Even when God launched his prophetic ministry, he remained in the desert. He was fully alive there. He didn't stay because he was a social outcast, but because the desert gave him an intimacy with God he never wanted to lose. He didn't leave the desert until he was carried to jail and killed. There's life in the desert with Jesus. There's death in the world without Him.

In the desert, all you have is God. He is all you ever need.

So what does a personally revived Christian look like?

They're pure, devoted, and fearless. They're loyal to God and keep His commands. They cling to the cross and long for the return of Christ. While others let their love for the Lord, their brothers and sisters, and their enemies wax cold, they love with intensity.

They love truth, speak truth, and stand for truth. They stand stalwart against doubt and unbelief. They walk by faith and not by sight. They're militant against lies and deception. They courageously swim against the tide of the world's philosophies, movements, and culture.

While others are asleep to prayer, they're mighty prayer warriors. They're awake when others are asleep—and hungry for God when others don't care. They pursue lives of holiness when other believers are steeped in compromise.

Revived Christians sing an octave too high, exasperating other believers living comfort-zone Christianity. They're talked about and falsely accused. They're labeled as legalistic, fanatical, and extreme. But they pay no mind to their critics because they're overcomers! They'll never let anyone extinguish their fire.

They're living, breathing, walking revivals—setting everything they touch ablaze for God. They're signs and wonders in the hands of Almighty God. They start fires wherever they go and will help usher in the greatest harvest this world has ever seen. They have a holy desperation for God and view the spiritual desert as a tremendous opportunity to thirst after Jesus.

They've been tried and tested and proven faithful. They're true biblical Christians. They're believers who have been personally revived.

How do you know you're thirsty for Jesus? When you don't care if you ever leave the desert—because you found intimacy with Jesus there. That's how you'll feel about this journey to personal revival. You won't want it to end.

Jesus is revival.

Questions for Reflection

→ Why do you need personal revival?

→ How thirsty are you for Jesus?

→ Are you willing to be a desert dweller to thirst for Jesus?

Prayer for Personal Revival

Lord, I cry out to You for personal revival.

Forgive me for being lukewarm.

I commit to setting apart the next 31 days to seek You until I find You.

Jesus, I'm holy desperate for more of You. Give me an unquenchable

thirst for You. Lord, set my heart on fire and flood me with Your Spirit.

I want more of You! I want to live a burning, shining, radical,

passionate Christian life. Help me live a lifestyle of revival.

Each day, as I focus on a different aspect of my Christian walk,

breathe life into that area and awaken it to You.

I won't stop until I achieve personal revival.

I love You, Lord! In Jesus' name I pray.

Amen.

DAY 2

Thirsty for First Love

REVELATION 2:1–7

> **LOOK BACK:** Yesterday you made the decision to pursue personal revival with everything in you. Today, as you embark on the next foundation stone of your journey, reaffirm that commitment to the Lord.

Imagine a man standing in a room listening to rousing music. His foot taps to the beat, his torso sways, and he breaks out in dance. It's apparent to everyone watching that he thoroughly enjoys the music.

Next, a deaf man enters the room. He observes the delight of the first man and desires the same experience. So the deaf man mimics the first man's every move. In the beginning, he remains awkward and clumsy, but with practice begins to mirror the first man's actions.

At first, there seems to be little distinction between the two dancing men. But upon closer examination, a huge disparity exists: the first man is responding to the beautiful music, while the deaf man is merely imitating the first man.

I think I know the deaf man. *He's me.*

Sadly, there have been seasons of my Christian walk when I caught myself going through the spiritual motions. On the surface an onlooker would never be able to tell because I still spoke Christianese, checked off my devotional boxes, and worked hard at being a good Martha for Jesus. But somewhere along the way, I'd lost my first love—just like the church in Ephesus.

Revelation 2–3 presents five churches in desperate need of revival—including the church in Ephesus. The Ephesian Christians had lost their first love. Though they vivaciously danced for the cause of Christ, they stopped hearing the music. Their love for Jesus dissipated. In this letter, they receive a severe rebuke from the Lord, who warns of dire consequences if they don't repent.

Rewind several decades earlier. In Acts 19, the church in Ephesus was in the throes of revival. The gospel was preached, with multitudes saved and missionaries sent forth. In addition, churches were planted, miracles performed, and hearts gripped by the fear of the Lord. The Ephesian believers repented of their sins, even to the point of burning expensive magic arts paraphernalia in a common bonfire. To show their love for Jesus, no price was too great. They were passionately in love with Jesus and utterly sold out to Him. What a picture of Christians in revival!

The Ephesians started out like the first dancing man (Acts 19). However, over time they lost their first love and shifted into form (Rev. 2). If it could happen to the church in Ephesus, it should be a "danger ahead" sign to all of us.

And here's the strange thing: if Jesus drops from greatest love status, He doesn't hold second place. He plummets to number 435 on our agape barometer. If Jesus isn't our top priority, He falls straight to the bottom. Crazy, but true.

> *Jesus is either our first love—or He's not.*
> *There's no in-between.*

So how in the world does this happen? I mean, how does a Christian go from "no price too great to show my love for Jesus" to "my love for Jesus has died a lukewarm death"?

The obvious answers are sin, compromise, worldliness, not guarding your eye and ear gates, etc. However, I have found that it's the not-so-recognizable love extinguishers that are the biggest detriments to my love for Jesus. Here are ten "first-love" questions that help me rekindle my love for Jesus. Prayerfully use them to examine your heart:

1. Have I become so familiar with Jesus that I've taken His redemptive work on the cross for granted?

2. Have I become apathetic, in any manner, toward my relationship with God?

3. Have I let distractions crowd my heart and diminish my love for Jesus?

4. Have I reduced my quiet time with Jesus to a time slot in my bloated schedule?

5. Have I let the cares of this world cause my passion for Jesus to become dull?

6. Have I let hardness of heart creep in?

7. Have I shifted my focus from loving Jesus to working for Jesus?

8. Have I lost my simple devotion to Jesus by complicating my Christian walk?

9. Have I become so battle weary that I no longer enjoy my relationship with Jesus?

10. Have I lost the wonder I had for Jesus when I first became born-again?

Is the Holy Spirit convicting you today? He is me! *Run* into the arms of our merciful God and fall in love with Him all over again. Ask Him to awaken the passion that was once ablaze in your heart.

I don't know about you, but these questions really trouble me. I hope they always do.

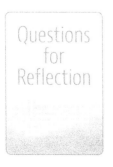
Questions for Reflection

→ What spoke the loudest to you from Revelation 2:1–7?

→ Which "first-love" question troubles you the most?

→ Is Jesus your first love?

Prayer for Personal Revival

Lord, revive my love for You.

I've let my love for You grow cold. Please forgive me.

I recognize I've become apathetic and complacent in my Christian walk.

I repent for letting routine and distractions crowd my life.

From this point on, I'll shift my focus to You. I want to return to a pure, simple devotion to You. Lord, restore the joy of my salvation and renew a right spirit within me. Renew the wonder I had for You when I was a new Christian. Please convict me if my love for You ever grows cold again. Remind me to always search my heart for anything that gets in the way of my white-hot love for You.

I love You, Lord! In Jesus' name I pray.

Amen.

DAY 3

Thirsty for Truth

2 CHRONICLES 34

> **LOOK BACK:** Yesterday Jesus returned to first-love status in your life. Ask Him to convict you if your love for Him ever begins to grow cold. Spend time lavishing your love on Him.

I could've eaten the pages of my Bible.

Well, not literally. Let me explain.

When I became a Christian at 26 years old, I had zero knowledge of the Scriptures. I was a clean slate. No exaggeration. I didn't even know the basic children's Bible stories of Adam and Eve or Noah and the ark. (I thought David and Goliath was a story about a boy and his dog!)

But there I was, a brand-new believer, wanting to know everything about the newfound Love of my life. I wanted to know the One who miraculously set me free from sin. I wanted to know the Way. I wanted to know the Life.

And I wanted to know the Truth.

Truth be told, I was starving for Truth.

My life had been built on one lie after the next; I believed whatever the world told me. It felt like I had plopped myself on a raft in the lazy river (there's one in every water park) and let the philosophies and ideologies of this world take me wherever. Up and down. Around and around. Upside down. This direction and that. Just never right-side up.

When I discovered the Word of God, I couldn't get enough. The answers I'd searched for my entire life were found on the pages of this Book. Some people read their Bible like a court document. I read it like a love letter.

The mirror of the Word helps me become more like Jesus. The hammer of Scripture broke self off of me, and the lamp of the Word directed my every step. I read the Word of God like it was liquid honey dripping from heaven, bathing my soul in God's agape love.

It was.

I determined that the Word would be the foundation of my life. I was so resolute that I placed a Bible in the foundation of our newly built home. I embedded a bonded-leather, brown Bible in the cement when our basement was poured. Not in a weird rabbit's foot kind of way, but in a let's-get-some-things-settled kind of way: the Truth of God's Word would always be the foundation of our family.

Then life went on. Work. Soccer practice. Ministry. Favorite TV show. Helping with homework. Time with friends. "Did you practice your piano?" Dinner prep. Financial woes. Health problems. Barely keeping my head above water. And I heard myself at times saying, "Wait a minute, I know it's here somewhere. I think the last time I saw my Bible was . . . er . . . umm. . . . "

Hence.

The Christian's drug of choice.

Busy.

An unthinkable reality happened. There were days I found myself too busy to read my Bible. Has this ever happened to you? Let me restate this question: has this *not* ever happened to you?

I know you've been waiting for it. So, to not disappoint, here it is:

If you're too busy to spend time in God's Word, you're too busy.

Mic drop!

On days like this, whether we'd like to admit it or not, our walk with God begins to spiral downward—even just a smidgeon. But as soon as we realize it, we need to intentionally rediscover God's Word, like King Josiah and the Israelites did in 2 Chronicles 34.

King Josiah was a godly ruler in a line of very wicked kings. He took the throne from his grandfather Manasseh, the most wicked ruler of them all. Exhibit A: during Manasseh's reign, he filled the land with pagan altars built to false gods. As a result, the Israelites completely turned their backs on God.

When Josiah became king, he gave orders to smash to smithereens the demonic altars his grandfather had built—and then restore the temple, which was now in utter ruin. While the workers repaired the temple, they stumbled upon the Book of the Law in the midst of the rubble. It had been lost for more than 50 years and—wait for it—*they didn't even know it was missing!*

After they rediscovered God's Word, Josiah made a bold move. He called all the Israelites together, from far and wide, and read the Book of the Law out loud. (Imagine if your pastor did that. Four chapters in, half the congregation would be asleep.) Josiah outlawed the worship of false gods and led the Israelites in rededication back to God.

Ahh . . . to have a radical love for the Word of God like Josiah. *We can!*

Whether you've let busyness overtake you, or you've lost sight of the magnificent gift God has given in the Bible, personal revival can transpire when you rediscover the Word of God.

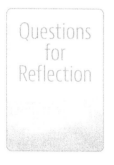

Questions for Reflection

→ Do you struggle to spend time in God's Word?

→ How is hunger for the Word of God related to personal revival?

→ Once lost, how do you regain an appetite for the Word?

Prayer for Personal Revival

Lord, revive my hunger for the Word.

I long for a deep, abiding love for the Bible. Give me fresh eyes

to see Your Word as the richest treasure known to man.

Help me value Your Word more than the food I eat.

Give me revelation of the spiritual strength and life it imparts.

Identify areas of my life where I have let busyness, distractions,

or the cares of this world impede my time in the Word of God.

Give me a voracious appetite for Scripture—one that will

never be satisfied. And help me never to underestimate,

devalue, or dismiss the power of the written Word of God.

May I devour it all the days of my life.

In Jesus' name I pray.

Amen.

DAY 4

Thirsty for a Soft Heart

MARK 6:45–52

> **LOOK BACK:** Yesterday your thirst for the Word of God was revived. Spend time thanking God that His Truth is your anchor. Today, recommit to reading it, mediating on it, and studying it.

"Your heart has layers and layers of callouses."

This was God's response after pouring out my painful heart to Him.

I had just experienced a year of traumatic events, one more hurtful than the other. There were challenges I'd never faced, a series of turbulent situations, and a succession of surprise attacks from the enemy. It felt like I had been swept over Niagara Falls in a barrel, unable to tell which end was up.

Physically, a callous appears on our bodies when there is pressure on an area of our skin, causing a hard surface to form. I have a callous on my finger from gripping my pen too tight when I write. Callouses protect our skin. We're fearfully and wonderfully made by our Creator.

Spiritually, however, hardness of heart can transpire from abrasive circumstances or suffering one hurt too many. Our hearts can also become calloused when we turn to someone or something besides God, searching for what only God can give. When we look to an idol, we turn away from Him. This hardens our hearts.

Symptoms of hardness of heart are many and varied. A calloused spiritual heart can manifest as passion loss, indifference, a feeling of numbness, or doubt. It is also noticeable when we isolate from people and God (isolation equals desolation), when our devotional time becomes dry and rote, or when we become jaded critics. Dire spiritual consequences can result from a hardened heart.

The disciples had just witnessed the miracle of feeding the 5,000. Immediately after, while they were in a boat on the Sea of Galilee, Jesus came walking on water toward them. The disciples were terrified of Him and cried out in fright. Mark 6:52 tells us why: ". . . for they still didn't understand the significance of the miracle of the loaves. Their hearts were too hard to take it in."

A hardened heart thwarts our spiritual understanding to the point that even miracles no longer impress. It's difficult to experience personal revival when our hearts are hard. No, it's downright impossible.

When God exposed my hardened heart that day, after recovering from the shock of my true heart condition, there were specific things I did to cooperate with God in softening my heart. These prayer directions served to give Him full access to my hardened heart. They saved my spiritual life.

Here are the eight steps I took to position myself for God's heart-softening. I implore you to go through them, one by one. Your spiritual life may depend upon them:

1. **Get honest with God.** Lay your heart on God's altar and pour it out to Him—*all of it.* Bring your bottled-up distress, questions, loss, habitual sin, lurking anxiety, anger, and unmet needs to the Lord. God can take it; His shoulders are broad. Get brutally honest with Him. Bring the contents of your heart into the light of Christ Jesus. Light chases darkness.

2. **Surrender your pain to Jesus.** If you don't, you'll build a memorial to those traumatic events, pitch a tent at its base, and camp out. No, instead give your hurts and disappointments to God and leave them there. God longs to turn your battle scars into beauty marks so that you reflect the image of our Savior.

3. **Extend forgiveness.** If you walked into a convenience store to buy a loaf of bread and the price tag read $100, would you buy it? Of course not. You would say, "That costs way too much!" Unforgiveness comes with an enormous price tag. It will weigh you down with a heavy emotional burden you were never intended to carry. But here is the highest price of all: if you don't forgive, you won't

be forgiven. Therefore, forgive whomever, whenever, of whatever. Forgive, let go of resentment, and repent of bitterness. And while you're at it, extend God's amazing grace to yourself as well.

4. **Intentionally cast your care upon the Lord.** Sometimes you barely catch your breath from one trial before you are afflicted with another. Therefore, it's vital to ensure you aren't shouldering the care of anything that has occurred. What problems or people are you still carrying? Picture yourself walking up to the throne of Jesus and placing your burdens in His hands: "Jesus, they're Yours."

5. **Ask God to perform spiritual heart surgery.** Our loving Heavenly Father wants to reach His healing hand into your spiritual heart to heal wounds, soften scar tissue, and tear down walls. Give Him permission to speak to your heart, convict your heart, strengthen your heart, and deposit the desires of *His* heart. Let God do a transforming work in your life by giving Him full access to your heart.

6. **Recalibrate your expectancy.** When you're sucker punched by the enemy, it's like you've experienced your own spiritual Pearl Harbor. This can deal a blow to your faith. If you aren't careful, your expectations of the future can reflect the hardships you've faced. Ask God to recalibrate your faith to echo Jeremiah 29:11: "'For I know the plans that I have for you,' says the Lord. 'They are plans for good and not for disaster, to give you a future and a hope.'"

7. **Refocus your vision.** Somewhere along the way of being turned upside down, your purpose probably got a little (or a lot) blurry. Prayerfully revisit your personal mission statement and let the Lord give you laser-focused vision. Ask Him to reignite your passion to continue running the race of your calling with reckless abandon.

8. **Learn every lesson.** Our lives are lived in seasons. And there are reasons for every season. Mine every lesson, revelation, and wisdom nugget you can from what you've just experienced. God is a multi-tasker and uses it all— the good, bad, and the ugly—to prepare us for His overall plan for our lives. Take everything you've learned in the wilderness into the next season of promise.

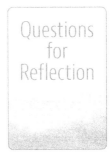

→ Are you presently experiencing symptoms of hardness of heart?

→ Are you struggling with a particular hurt?

→ Why do you think a hardened heart impedes personal revival?

Personal Prayer for Revival

Lord, I ask You to search my heart and expose any hard places.

I ask You to reach Your healing hands into my spiritual heart to smooth

any callouses and soften scar tissue. Tear down any walls I have built to

protect myself from future hurt. You are Lord of my life and Protector of

my heart. Open the eyes and ears of my heart so I can see and hear You.

Help me to guard my heart. I turn back to You in any area I may have

turned to an idol. Break up the fallow ground of my heart

so that I'll be thirsty for You once again.

I love You, Lord! In Jesus' name I pray.

Amen.

DAY 5

Thirsty to Surrender

LUKE 22:39–46

> **LOOK BACK:** Yesterday God softened the hard places of your heart. Your heart is where you live; your heart is where you love God. Ask God to help you keep watch over your heart so it continues to be soft, free, and pliable in His hands.

Warning: rant to follow!

One of the biggest frustrations of my Christian walk is this: to observe believers, those I have discipled for years, never get around to surrendering their lives to Christ. The signs are usually the same: the world still holds great attraction, there is general lack of commitment to all God-related things, and they live rollercoaster Christian lives.

Oh, they say they're Christians, that they love Jesus and live for Him. They say a lot of things. But generally speaking, their decisions benefit self. Christians aren't very Christian when they are self-absorbed.

Equally as frustrating is watching believers, who have spent a lifetime of surrender to God, throw it all away in a pivotal moment because they are unwilling to surrender that *one* thing to God. A person. A situation. Opportunities that were good ideas, but not God's will for them. Anything.

But want to know the frustration that tops all frustrations?

It's the times in *my life* when God asked *me* to surrender something, and I either harden my heart to His voice or make excuses for why it's not necessary.

Well, everyone has a weakness; this is mine.

After all, no one is perfect.

I've spent almost my entire life yielding all I have to the Lord; I deserve to keep this one thing for myself.

I live a more surrendered life than most Christians I know.

Idolatrous and ugly!

When I became a follower of Christ several decades ago, I promised the Lord, "I'm Yours. My life isn't my own. It's no longer about me. From this point on, it's all about You." My prayer of initial surrender wasn't a repeat-after-me-type prayer. No, it came from the deep recesses of my heart. But at times, rebellion has crept in unaware.

Our surrender to Christ happens initially as well as progressively. The moment we make a decision to follow Christ, we make a one-time, quality decision to surrender our entire lives to Christ. But surrender is also progressive. Every day, we need to surrender specific areas of our lives that don't align with God's will (my plan, worldly thinking, fleshly appetites, other loves, my rights, and on and on). If we spend a lifetime surrendering our will to the Father's will, we'll have lived a surrendered life unto the Lord.

So what is surrender? In short, it's this:

I have a will.

God has a will.

I relinquish my will to God's will.

Surrender is making Jesus Lord over a particular aspect of our lives in which we previously sought to be lord. It is abandoning to the Lord that space where we acted as self-appointed managers. Surrender means there is no aspect of life not submitted to Jesus as Lord.

Many believers live cafeteria-style Christian lives—they pick and choose what they surrender. When we dine at a buffet, we slide our trays down the line and say things like, "I'll take the roast beef, but hold the gravy. I want the carrots, but please no brussels sprouts. I'll have the apple pie, but hold the vanilla ice cream." But Jesus expects us to surrender 100 percent of our lives to Him.

The word "kingdom" literally means "king's domain." King Jesus holds ultimate authority in His Kingdom. His Kingdom isn't a democracy. We don't get to pick and choose what we like and don't like. When we become followers of Christ, we give King Jesus supreme authority over our lives.

So, what does a life completely yielded to God look like? *JESUS.*

The biblical account of Jesus in the Garden of Gethsemane, on the night of His arrest, clearly depicts a picture of surrender. "He walked away, about a stone's throw, and knelt down and prayed, 'Father, if you are willing, please take this cup of suffering away from me. Yet I want your will to be done, not mine'" (Luke 22:41–42).

Jesus surrendered to His Father. Was it difficult? *Yes.* Did He want to find another way? *Yes.* But did He relinquish His will to the Father's plan? *Yes.* Jesus knew that without Gethsemane there could be no Golgotha. And without Golgotha, there would be no resurrection.

We experience our own Gethsemane when we hold differing opinions, perhaps even profoundly different, to that of God's—yet we give up what we think is best. Surrender is agreeing with God's will for our lives no matter how much it hurts or what it costs.

Difficult? Yes. But for the follower of Christ, surrender is the only option. Anything else is idolatry.

A Gethsemane moment is God's invitation to His ultimate goal for our lives—resurrection. Resurrection life is only possible to the one who has first gone through Gethsemane.

If Jesus is truly Lord of your life, whatever God asks you to surrender is not up for negotiation. The answer is, "Yes, Lord, yes, to Your will and to Your way." This is the place of ultimate peace, freedom, and strength (the antithesis: fear, bondage, and weakness). This is the beauty and power of a fully surrendered life in Christ.

So, take stock of your life: relationships, finances, decision-making, body care, time management, work, play, sleep, marriage, parenting, etc. View them as segments of your life (like slices of a pie). Take each one before the Lord in prayer. To what extent have you given Jesus Lordship over these areas?

Surrendering to Christ is no minor thing—*it's everything.*

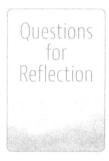

Questions for Reflection

→ What areas of your life have been difficult to surrender?

→ What was the result of a situation you didn't relinquish to God?

→ Are there any specific areas God is asking you to surrender to Him now?

Prayer for Personal Revival

Lord, search every part of me. What am I still holding on to?

What area of my life is Your finger on? I surrender all that I am

and all that I have. I place my life before You as an offering—

a living sacrifice—on Your altar. I acknowledge that You know best—always.

Show me areas of my life I'm not trusting You enough to surrender.

Forgive me. Lord, there are some parts of my life that are easier to

surrender than others. I'm having a hard time yielding these areas to You.

Please help me, Jesus. You're my Lord, King, and Master.

And from this point on, I'll live surrendered to You.

I love You, Lord! In Jesus' name I pray.

Amen.

DAY 6
Thirsty for Holiness

ISAIAH 6:1–9

> **LOOK BACK:** Yesterday you surrendered to God all you were withholding. What a relief! Make the decision that you won't take back what you relinquished. Today, once again, place your entire life on God's altar.

"HOLY, HOLY, HOLY. . ."

In heaven, of all the wonderful attributes of God that could be repeated over and over again, it is the word *HOLY.* Night and day, they never stop calling to one another *HOLY.* The sound of their voices saying *HOLY* makes thresholds and doorposts shake (Rev. 4, Isa. 6).

God is holy. Holy is He. Pure. Unblemished. Sinless. And God calls His people to live holy lives before Him.

When my son was in the sixth grade, he came home from school one day and asked me a question. This was our conversation:

Son: *Mom, can I watch (ungodly) TV show?*

Me: *No.*

Son: *When I'm 13 can I watch it?*

Me: *Nope.*

Son: *16?*

Me: *Definitely not.*

Son: *Then when can I watch it?*

Me: *You can't watch that show when you're 18, 28, 48, or even when you're 88.*

Son: *Why not?*

Me: *Because God is HOLY!*

Holiness isn't about a list of things we can't do. Absolutely everything is measured against the holiness of God. God Himself is the standard. He doesn't conform to our standard. We adapt to His. And His standard is always holiness. Period.

God hates sin like parents hate the terminal disease that ravages their baby's body. God and sin don't mix; Jesus and Satan have nothing in common. Therefore we're commanded to put away sin and live holy lives before Him. Scripture makes this abundantly clear:

> But now you must be holy in everything you do, just as God who chose you is holy. For the Scriptures say, "You must be holy because I am holy" (1 Peter 1:15-16).
>
> . . . work at living a holy life, for those who are not holy will not see the Lord (Heb. 12:14).
>
> . . . let us cleanse ourselves from everything that can defile our body or spirit. And let us work toward complete holiness because we fear God (2 Cor. 7:1).

Please stop believing the lie that sin satisfies. Only God satisfies. All of sin's promises are empty. As a matter of fact, when we partake of one kind of sin, it will give birth to more of the same—and more.

When we add a log to the fire of sin's altar, it produces an insatiable desire to add more and more logs. If not stopped, it will progress to adding logs just to get through our day. What started as "just this one time" will turn into "I can't live without it."

In the 1800s, pioneers in America loaded their wagon trains to head west in search of territory to settle. Once property was located, they asked, "Is this land above the 'snake line'?" Every mountain has an invisible line called the "snake line." Snakes don't like thin air. They live in the woodsy lowlands where they can easily hide.

Living below the snake line was considered foolish and unthinkable because it could lead to death. Pioneers didn't take snakes as pets, pay money to be entertained by snakes, take vacations in the lowlands, or allow their children to play at people's homes filled with snakes.

Jesus delivered us from sin and set us above sin's line. He calls His people to dwell in heavenly places. Why would we ever want to go back to living in the lowlands?

The enemy tempts us with sin and then blinds us to the consequences. Here's a consequence: sin is the access key Satan uses to unlock the door of our hearts. Here's another: when we sin, our filthy, dirty feet trample on the precious blood of Jesus that cost Him His life.

Here's yet another: when there is sin in our hearts, we won't come boldly to God's throne—which is an unfathomable privilege. Sin will rob us of confidence to stand before Almighty God; sin makes us feel uncomfortable in God's presence. We'll only draw as close to God as our level of holiness permits.

How can we live holy? First, it's important to understand that if God commands us to live holy, He equips us to do so. The blood of Jesus doesn't just forgive us of our sins, it empowers us not to sin. God never asks us to do something we can't do.

So, what is the key to living holy? What you behold, you become. Just like you'll never lose weight by staring at a box of donuts, you'll never become holy by staring at your sin.

Holiness is obtained by spending time at God's holy throne, gazing at holy God, and meditating on His holy Word.

When God encountered the prophet Isaiah (Isa. 6:1–9), he was overcome by God's holiness—and thus by his own sin. Have you ever heard the distinct, disturbing sound of a person who has just lost someone dear? Isaiah experienced that kind of intense grief over the repulsion of his sin: "It's all over! I am doomed, for I am a sinful man. I have filthy lips, and I live among a people with filthy lips . . ." (Isa. 6:5).

There are no shortcuts. In the holiness of God, everything is laid bare. Like Isaiah, God is encountering you with His holiness and beckoning you to live a holy life before Him. *HOLY, HOLY, HOLY.*

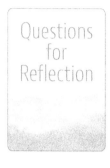

Questions for Reflection

→ Is there a sin that hinders you from holiness?

→ How does living in habitual sin impede personal revival?

→ Why do you think holiness is achieved by gazing at God and not our sin?

Prayer for Personal Revival

Lord, I know that holiness isn't a suggestion but a command.

Forgive me for treating the issue of sin so lightly.

There is nothing I desire more than to live a holy life before You.

God, encounter me with Your holiness! Holy God, help me

come into Your holy presence and gaze at Your holiness.

Give me a holy hatred for sin. Let me see the filthiness of my own sin.

Remind me to guard my heart and protect my eye and ear gates from sin.

I want to live a pure, strong, powerful, undiluted life before You.

Convict me if I'm ever again tempted to live in the lowlands of sin.

I love you, Lord! In Jesus' name I pray.

Amen.

DAY 7

Thirsty for Repentance

2 CORINTHIANS 7:8–13

> **LOOK BACK:** Yesterday God encountered you with His holiness. Today, make the decision to live above the "snake line." Start by entering God's throne room. Gaze at holy God and meditate on His holy Word.

Let me make something abundantly clear right out of the gate:

God never tires of your voice asking for mercy.

This applies to the one-and-done mercy prayers, as well as the prayers of "I've asked for forgiveness for the same sin more times than I can count." God doesn't want you to languish in guilt or shame when you've sinned, but to run immediately into His loving arms. The enemy, however, wants you to think otherwise. He'll whisper in your ear, "God's weary of your repeated cries for forgiveness."

God is rich in mercy. Mercy is who God is. He yearns to lavish His mercy on you, scrub you clean with His blood, and restore you to new creation status—just as if you never sinned. Forgiveness is yours for the asking. However, God wants to do a deeper work in your heart through the grace of repentance.

"Repent" was the first word John the Baptist spoke in his forerunner ministry (Matt 3:2), the first word of Jesus in His public ministry (Matt. 4:17), and remains an elementary doctrine of Christ (Heb. 6:1). In five out of the seven letters to the churches in Revelation, Jesus tells the churches to repent (Rev. 2–3). The message of repentance is a major theme in both the Old and New Testaments.

To repent means to turn away from sin by doing a spiritual "about face" or making a 180-degree change of direction. At one time, you were headed toward your sin. But because you've repented, you walk the complete opposite way. Let me illustrate using my struggle with the habitual sin of gluttony.

I battled gluttony most of my adult life. I was delivered from alcoholism 32 years ago when I was born again, so instead I ate—and ate and ate. Sugar is cheap, legal, and readily available. It gave me a high by spiking my blood sugar and making my heart race. I was a full-blown sugar addict. I ate sweets when sad, frustrated, angry, and discouraged—when experiencing any type of negative emotion. It was how I coped with stress, and I was stressed a lot.

Overeating is one of the few sins you wear like a coat for all to see. I felt like the scarlet letter "G" for gluttony was embroidered on my shirt. I was so ashamed. Shame acts like a tape recorder in your mind, reminding you over and over of your failure. I was in a dangerous, never-ending cycle of pain, gluttony, shame, pain, gluttony, shame, and on and on and on. For years I repeatedly asked God to forgive me.

But by God's grace, I came to the place where I saw gluttony for what it was: an idol that had to be smashed. Every sin is an idol. An idol is what we look to, instead of turning to God. Sin creates intimacy with the idol; repentance creates intimacy with God. Repentance is the exit ramp off idol worship, and the on-ramp to the presence of Almighty God.

Therefore I had to repent from the sin of gluttony. This consisted of more than just muttering a prayer of forgiveness under my breath during a commercial break, only to reach for more food at the next commercial. I had to truly repent. I also knew that without repentance, I wouldn't experience personal revival. Sustained personal revival transpires in a Christian who lives a lifestyle of repentance.

So here is the process of repentance that I undertook. These steps can be applied to any sin with which you struggle:

- **Take your sin before the Lord**. Lay it out all out before Him. He already knows, but do it anyway. Pour your heart out before Almighty God. Share your heartfelt desire to receive freedom from the sin that binds. Tell God you want nothing to get in the way of intimacy with Him or from experiencing personal revival. Communicate your love for Him!

- **Ask God to give you godly sorrow.** When we sin, we sin against God and God alone. Hurting God should cause us to grieve over sin. When it doesn't, something is spiritually wrong. 2 Corinthians 7:10 says, "For the kind of sorrow God wants us to experience leads us away from sin. . . . But worldly sorrow, which lacks repentance, results in spiritual death."

- **Ask for forgiveness.** Tell God you're sorry for turning to idols instead of running to Him. Express your pain for saying, "I love you, God," one moment, and then sinning against Him the next. Pour your grief out to Him for desiring the things of this world more than you desire Him; for loving your sin more than you love Him. Tell Him you're sorry for falling into deception and believing the enemy's lies. Ask Him to forgive you for repetitively crying out for mercy with absolutely no intention of laying down your sin.

- **Turn away from your sin.** In old western movies, bandits would take captive entire villages. They would load every person onto a covered wagon, and right before pulling away, would give their captives one last look at their village. With tears streaming down the captives' faces, they would watch their village burn to the ground. Why did the bandits do this? So that the captives would know there was nothing to go back to. When we repent, we turn away from our sin, never looking back. There is nothing to go back to but pain, misery, and death.

- **Ask God for restoration.** Sin leads to death—death of relationships, mental and physical health, finances, dreams, hopes, peace, and our friendship with God. Sin will lie and tell you that you're the exception to the rule. (You aren't!) However, the Great Restorer wants to restore all that was stolen. Restoration is always God's end-goal. Ask Him to repair and rebuild the effect that sin had on your life. Ask Him for personal revival.

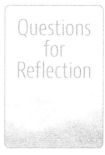

Questions for Reflection

→ Have you ever believed the lie that you're the exception to the effects of sin?

→ Has God revealed any sins from which you need to repent?

→ What is the difference between godly sorrow and worldly sorrow over sin?

Prayer for Personal Revival

Lord, search my heart and reveal every part that has been

contaminated by sin. Expose every sin in my life so I can repent.

Give me a heart that is quick to repent and quick to obey.

Soften my heart so I'll be sensitive to the conviction of the

Holy Spirit. Show me sin from Your perspective so that

I'll feel godly sorrow, leading to repentance.

I want nothing to stand in the way of my relationship with You.

I want personal revival. I'm so grateful that You are rich in mercy.

Have mercy on me, Lord. I love You, Lord!

In Jesus' name I pray.

Amen.

DAY 8

Thirsty for Joy

NEHEMIAH 8:10

> **LOOK BACK:** Yesterday God gave the roadmap to genuine repentance. Today, ask God to examine your heart for hidden sin. Review the steps to repentance. As this day continues, make the decision that you'll be quick to repent if you sin. God is rich in mercy.

Joy is no small thing.

We tend to minimize joy, like how I view a maraschino cherry on top of an ice cream sundae. A cherry is great finish to a sundae, but if it's missing, it's no big deal. Joy isn't optional or non-essential to our Christian walk. As a matter of fact, it acts as a barometer of our spiritual strength, because . . .

. . . the joy of the LORD is your strength (Neh. 8:10).

Much joy = much strength. Little joy = little strength. I repeat, joy is no small thing, especially as it pertains to personal revival. A revived believer is strong in the Lord because he or she has fullness of joy. Jesus is his or her joy. In stark contrast, when Christians lose their joy, it signals something is very amiss, like an automobile's check-engine light.

My first car was a boxy, cocoa-brown 1976 Ford Granada—aka—The Lemon. The beige interior smelled like mildew and Armor All (used to cover up the musty smell). My mom purchased it from her coworker two weeks before my driver's test so it would be ready and waiting when the big day arrived.

With license in tow and a grin from ear-to-ear, I headed down the road to start my new life of independence—for about a mile. The Lemon quickly overheated. The car apparently had an oil leak; the dipstick was bone dry. My badge of newfound freedom turned into a crash course on teenage auto mechanics.

What oil is to a car, joy is to our relationship with God. A dry oil tank will cause a car engine to burn up. Joylessness Christianity is infinitely more dangerous. Without joy, we'll burn out, wear out, or give out. We need to pay close attention to our joy levels.

Joy isn't a feeling. Feelings are fleeting and fickle. Happiness is a feeling that originates in the mind. Happiness is encrusted with external and temporary adornments. Joy and happiness are completely different.

Joy is of the heart and is a byproduct of the pursuit of Christ. It's a fruit of the Spirit (Gal. 5:22–23) and originates from the throne of God. Joy comes giftwrapped in contentment, beauty, and trust. It can bloom right next to grief, loneliness, or disappointment—and starve whatever negative emotions are near.

We can't lather up joy. It's a choice. Our joy grows when we have the opportunity not to be joyous—but are joyful anyway. Joy diminishes when we're enticed to cast our joy aside, and give temptation sway.

Here's something startling: the spiritual maturity of a Christian can be measured by what it takes to steal his or her joy. *Ow!* A Christian of any maturity level can experience joy right smack dab in the middle of a miracle. Who can't do that? But the revived Christian also lives with joy between miracles. Between the miracles is where the authentic Christian walk is lived.

To fix The Lemon's oil leak, I had to find where the leak originated. Same with joy. We can find ourselves joyless, but completely unaware how we arrived at that condition. That's why it's important to recognize "joy leaks."

I've experienced "joy leaks" when:

- I had my eyes on my circumstances.

- I stopped being eternity-minded.

- I put ministry to others before ministry to God.

- I ceased doing everything unto the Lord, and my motive became anything else.

- I chose discouragement in lieu of joy.

- I allowed fear, doubt, or unbelief in my heart. Faith and joy are partners.

- I stopped walking in my purpose.

- I had unrepentant sin in my heart.

- I focused on self instead of others.

- I wasn't casting all my cares upon the Lord.

Do you recognize any of these "joy leaks" in your Christian walk? If so, run to the foot of the cross, stop the joy drains through repentance, and ask God to restore the joy of your salvation.

Maintain your joy though the hordes of hell attack from every angle. Joy responds to every matter of life from a heavenly perspective. In fact, when we walk in the joy of the Lord, we get a foretaste of heaven.

When miracles delay, your joy will stay.

Jesus is your joy.

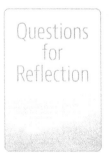

Questions for Reflection

→ Between 1–10, how would you rate your present level of joy?

→ Which "joy leaks" resonate with you the most?

→ How can you periodically and intentionally check your joy level?

Prayer for Personal Revival

Lord, I'm spiritually dry. I've lost my joy. Jesus,

You are my Strength, my Song, and my Salvation.

You are my Joy!

Help me to count it all joy when I face adversity of every kind.

Help me to live with joy between the miracles.

Restore the joy of my salvation and renew a right spirit within me.

From this day forward, I choose joy because I choose You.

Teach me to respond to every matter of life from

a heavenly perspective and see You at work in all things.

Convict me if I experience a "joy leak" so I can repent.

Thank You for letting Your fountain of joy flow once again in my life.

I love You, Lord! In Jesus' name I pray.

Amen.

DAY 9

Thirsty to Sit at Jesus' Feet

LUKE 10:38–42

> **LOOK BACK:** Yesterday your joy was revived. *Hallelujah!* Today, make the choice to live joyous, regardless of your circumstances. Ask God to help you guard against "joy leaks." Respond to all of today's events from the perspective of heaven.

It was the night before my father's funeral. My dad had just lost a long health battle and my heart was broken. Fraught with grief, I was desperate for consolation and healing. Barely able to think, I ran to the feet of Jesus.

With Bible open, I began worshiping God in the quiet of the night. With tears streaming down my face, I spilled my hurting heart out to Him. I could sense His gentle, comforting presence. His healing arms enveloped me.

"Lord," I whispered, "I want every aspect of my father's funeral to bring You glory." I could feel the burden of God's heart constrain mine. Although I was a young believer, I discerned God's concern for the unsaved who would be in attendance at my dad's service.

The Lord responded to my heart's cry: "I want you to speak."

Thinking God might have misunderstood (like God could possibly make a mistake), I reworded my question, "Lord, when people say, 'I'm so sorry for your loss,' how should I answer?" God repeated Himself: "I want you to speak." After the second time, I knew exactly what He was telling me to do.

The next morning, with knees buckling and voice quivering, I gripped the podium at the funeral home and publicly presented the gospel at my dad's service. It was one of those out-of-season, walk-on-water-with-Jesus events of my life. I was beyond grateful I'd spent time at the feet of Jesus the night before.

In that secret place, God comforted me, poured His liquid love upon me, and imparted to me His passion for souls. In addition, God assigned me with the most difficult thing I had ever done (at the time), granted me the grace to obey, and healed my broken heart—all in one clean swoop. Without a doubt, this event caused me to cherish sitting at Jesus' feet more than ever before. The reason I share this story is this:

> *Your daily, divine appointment with God*
> *is the solitary most important event of your day.*

Every morning, I go to my prayer nook to spend time with my Savior. With sunlight streaming through my windows, and the occasional view of a blue jay perching on its feeder, I focus my attention on Jesus and draw near to Him. Curled up on my striped, overstuffed "prayer chair," I reach for my Bible, pen, and prayer journal, and begin feasting on the living Word of God.

Then I talk to God using words that one would with a dear friend of 32 years. I usually start like this: "Lord, I've come to meet with You. Share Your heart with me."

I sit in silence, giving Him time and space to speak. Then I share my heart with Him. He talks to me. And I talk to Him. And He talks to me. And I talk to Him. And day-by-day, daily devotion after daily devotion, I'm cultivating an intensely personal, passionate relationship with Almighty God.

Neglecting your hidden life with Jesus will generate more problems than you can possibly imagine; your Christian walk will quickly begin to decay. This is why the enemy attacks your time with God: "You deserve a break today." "Turn on the television and relax." "Call your friend to vent." "You can't pray after what you've done." "You have too much to do." "Go back to sleep."

The enemy knows that when you make your daily devotions a habit, you establish habitual dependence on God. He knows that your doubts and fears will suffocate, and you'll receive the love, peace, and mercy that lesser things could never provide. When you spend concentrated time with Jesus, your flesh, rebellion, and pride are put to death. Ungodly desires will melt away and you'll obtain everything you need for life and godliness.

But most importantly, when you set time aside each day with the Lord, you experience Him. Developing a deep a relationship with the Pearl of Great Price, the Bright Morning Star, and the Lily of the Valley is the reward. And it whets your appetite for more of Him. Time spent with God causes us to crave more of God.

Friend, please remember this: the world, with all of its glitz and glamour, is incapable of quenching the thirst of your soul. It promises much but delivers nothing. It's dry as a bone. When you turn to that which is void of life, you become lifeless still. We only experience life when we spend time with Life.

Little did sisters Martha and Mary know they would go down in Bible history as the poster children of daily devotions. Martha was famous for letting distractions thwart her time with Jesus (oh, God, please don't ever let me be famous for that), and Mary became known for her commitment to sitting at Jesus' feet.

Martha took great issue with Jesus for letting Mary "just sit there" while she prepared dinner. The more our lives are go-go-go, the more self-important we become. *The world can't possibly function without me if I spend one hour with Jesus.* Busyness and self-importance go hand-in-hand.

Jesus answered Martha's "it's not fair" complaint like this: "My dear Martha, you are worried and upset over all these details! There is only one thing worth being concerned about. Mary has discovered it, and it will not be taken away from her" (Luke 10:41–42).

Determine today to renew your commitment to sit at the feet of Jesus. Rediscover the one thing that matters. Make whatever adjustments are needed to keep your daily appointment with Him. You need Him as much today as when you were a brand-new believer. The greater someone's spiritual maturity, the more the realization that spending daily time with Jesus isn't optional, but a necessity.

Questions for Reflection

→ Do you relate more to Martha or Mary?

→ Describe your daily devotional time.

→ How can you become more devoted to sitting at Jesus' feet?

Prayer for Personal Revival

Lord, stoke the ember of my devotional life.

As I sit at Your feet, set me on fire for You, and then use me to

set the world on fire. God, I recommit myself to spending quality,

quiet time with You every day. There is nothing I desire more than an

intimate, deep, love relationship with You. When the enemy tempts me to

shift my focus on someone or something else, remind me that only You

can quench my thirst. Convict me if I'm tempted to skip my daily time with

You or become too busy or distracted. I know that as I draw near to You,

You will draw near to me. While I know there are vast blessings when

I meet with You, more than anything, it's You I long to experience.

I love You, Lord! In Jesus' name I pray.

Amen.

DAY 10

Thirsty for Prayer

ACTS 4:23–31

> **LOOK BACK:** Yesterday Jesus beckoned you to His feet every day. Here you are, once more, at His feet. Your decision will affect eternity! Today, as you draw near to God, expect Him to draw near to you. Enjoy your time in His presence as God revives your prayer time.

Our immune systems are marvelous creations of God. When they are strong and working properly, optimal health ensues. Disease is eradicated before one symptom appears. When we have a robust immune system, our energy levels are high and we're full of life.

But when someone's immune system is compromised, they're vulnerable to illness, experience frequent infections, and heal much more slowly. They can also feel weak, become fatigued, and experience weight loss. Immune deficiency can lead to loss of life.

Prayer is the immune system of the follower of Christ.

Without a consistent prayer life, our relationship with God will be anemic and shallow. We'll become spiritually emaciated and will lose our appetite for things of God. Without a vibrant prayer life, weakness will overtake us and make us defenseless against the attacks of the enemy. We'll fall into a spiritual slumber. Prayerlessness is a killer disease to our Christian walk.

But when Christians possess a robust prayer life, they can experience personal revival. It's in the place of prayer where the Holy Spirit—in the fireplace of our hearts—lights our fire for God. It's through prayer we cultivate a hunger and thirst for God, providing life-giving oxygen to keep burning for Him. But when our prayer times are erratic, our fire for God is dampened.

Prayer can't be the sideshow for the believer who desires personal revival. It must be the main event. When we come to God in prayer, we create a place where the Holy Spirit is welcome. God responds to asking, and prayer is the place we ask God to pour His Spirit upon our thirsty hearts. Prayer also makes the difference between the rain of the Holy Spirit falling on hearts of either concrete or thirsty ground.

Prayer is our way of cooperating with God to create a big enough reservoir in our hearts to contain an outpouring of God's Spirit. Prayer increases our capacity to receive more of Him. And as we cry out to God, He breaks us, shapes us, and gets us to the point of deeper desperation and dependency on Him.

Prayer precedes personal revival, undergirds personal revival, sustains personal revival, and produces Christians who pray for corporate revival. One believer, whose heart has been set on fire in personal revival, can ignite a million candles of revival through prayer. All it takes is one flame.

I want to be that flame, and I'm fully persuaded that you do as well. That's why you're reading this book.

The Book of Acts is a portrait of Christians in the throes of revival. It's interesting to note that the Bible records more than 650 prayers, and the Book of Acts contains more references to prayer than perhaps any other Book. This demonstrates the strong correlation between prayer and revival.

We find in Acts:

- Prayer birthed the Church (Acts 2:1–4).

- The first Christians devoted themselves to prayer (Acts 2:42).

- They protected prayer from the busyness of their harried schedule (Acts 6:1–4).

- They gave themselves constantly to prayer (Acts 1:14).

- Prayer was the environment in which the Holy Spirit poured Himself out (Acts 2:1–4, 8:15, 10:9–13, 30).

- There are 30 references to prayer.

- There were 14 corporate prayer meetings.

- Prayer was the breath of the early Church.

- Christians were walking revivals because of prayer.

If we desire personal revival, we need to prioritize prayer in the same way. The connection between prayer and revival in the Book of Acts clearly establishes that prayer needs to be the focal point of our lives. Nothing else will generate the same results.

However, the primary motive of our prayers needs to be this: *I want more of Jesus.* Any prayer that comes from a motive of wanting more of Jesus is a biblical prayer for personal revival. Any revival prayer that is self-driven with the intention of making up for our deficiencies or to somehow improve our lives, isn't a biblical revival prayer.

Acts 4:23–31 illustrates the value these new Christians placed on the place of prayer, as well as the power of God that is generated from the place of prayer. After hearing that Peter and John were released from prison for preaching the gospel, the believers lifted their voices in prayer. This was the result: "After this prayer, the meeting place shook, and they were all filled with the Holy Spirit. Then they preached the word of God with boldness" (Acts 4:31).

The Holy Spirit made His manifest presence visibly seen and felt as the early believers gathered in prayer. Through their room-shaking prayer, God filled them with His Spirit, enabling them to preach the Word of God with boldness. When we pray, God's power is released from heaven. Our prayers go up, and God's power comes down. Conversely, if our prayers don't go up, God's power doesn't come down.

God longs to bring His lukewarm, backslidden, spiritually asleep, and apathetic children back to life. Let's partner with Him in prayer, first for personal revival, then for the revival of our family, church, region, and nation. And as we cry out to God in prayer, let's live in expectation of the revival God so desperately wants to send!

Questions
for
Reflection

→ Read and meditate on Acts 4:23–31.
   What impacted you the most?

→ Would you say you have a passion for prayer
   and intercession?

→ Share a time when God miraculously
   answered a prayer.

Prayer for Personal Revival

Lord, revive my prayer life.

Reignite my times of prayer with a fresh grace.

I'm so grateful that Your ear is always attentive to my cries.

Help me to never take the privilege, honor, or responsibility

of prayer for granted. I want to be devoted to prayer and constant in

prayer. Help me to protect my prayer life from the busyness of life.

I also ask You to give me a revelation of the power of corporate prayer

with my brothers and sisters in Christ. Lord, I want my prayers to be big,

bold, and global. Although I desire personal revival,

I also ask You for worldwide revival. Jesus, I want more of You.

You are revival! I love You, Lord! In Jesus' name I pray.

Amen.

DAY 11
Thirsty for Fasting

MATTHEW 6:1–18

LOOK BACK: Yesterday God breathed His breath of life into your prayer life. Today, determine to pray big, bold, and global prayers. Ask God to make you continually thirsty for more of Him in the place of prayer.

Jesus is our example for every matter of life. As followers of Christ, we do what He does. When Jesus walked the earth He fasted. That's really all we need to know. Jesus fasted, therefore we should fast.

In the Sermon on the Mount, Jesus gives fasting instructions. He begins His teaching: "But *when* you fast . . ." (Matt. 6:17, emphasis added). Notice He didn't say, "But *if* you fast . . ." Comparatively, Jesus uses the same words regarding giving and prayer: "But *when* you give . . ." (Matt. 6:3) and "But *when* you pray . . ." (Matt. 6:6). It is a given that Christians fast, just as it is assumed believers will also give and pray. Fasting is normal Christianity.

The early Church was committed to fasting and prayer. History informs that Christians in the Book of Acts fasted an average of two days per week. Prayer, coupled with fasting, birthed and sustained the greatest move of God this world has ever seen. Yet, fasting remains the most undervalued, underemphasized, and underutilized spiritual treasure in today's Church.

I've conducted periodic fasts my entire Christian walk. Before I fast, I ask God what type and length of fast He would have me undertake. I've fasted one meal, two meals, a half-day (waiting until 3:00 p.m.), 24-hour, three days, ten days, and the Daniel fast (fruits, vegetables, and grains). I have Christian friends who have conducted 21-day and 40-day fasts. (Remember to consult your doctor before starting any type of fast. If you can't fast for medical reasons, fast and pray between meals.)

My reasons for fasting are many and varied, but include:

- for needed breakthrough
- to regain spiritual hunger
- to humble myself before God
- when making a major life decision
- when I'm struggling with submitting to God's will
- when I'm reverting back to religion from relationship
- to give teeth to repentance
- to get my cutting edge back in prayer
- when I'm feeling overwhelmed
- when embarking on a new year or endeavor
- to clearly hear God's voice
- to ready myself for the return of Christ
- for personal revival.

I had Lyme disease for 15 long years. It was a fiery trial that seemed to go on with no end in sight. I awoke every single morning to flu-like symptoms, but had an entire day's activities ahead. I was a full-time wife, mom, employee, and ministry worker. There were many days I couldn't put one foot in front of the other. However, I stood on God's promises and relied on His strength and grace to see me through.

One particular day, in agony and desperation, I cried out to the Lord for help. I felt like I couldn't take it any more. After I prayed, I felt impressed to go on a three-day fast that I began the next morning. Although I don't exactly know when my healing manifested, at the end of the three days, all my symptoms of Lyme disease had disappeared.

Why did it take 15 years for my healing to appear? Why did God choose to heal me during that particular three-day fast when I had fasted many times during the course of that painful season? I still don't know the answers to these questions. While I don't presume this is God's method for everyone battling chronic illness (we all have different relationships with God—His plan for each one of us is perfect), my day of breakthrough came during that fast. This I know for sure:

Fasting adds spiritual D-Y-N-A-M-I-T-E to our prayer lives.

Our days are filled with distractions and excess; fullness is dullness, but hunger is passion. When we fast, we deny ourselves the pleasure of food to gain greater intimacy with God. We don't fast to garner God's favor; this is something we already possess. Fasting helps us to align with God's will, plans and purposes, and to hunger after God more fully. When we empty ourselves, God will fill us.

Some helpful fasting pointers:

1. **Biblical fasting is giving up food.** Abstaining from TV or social media are fantastic ideas that can be coupled with fasting, but that's not fasting. Food is a base need; TV and social media aren't.

2. **Spiritually prepare before your fast.** Ask God to ready your heart. Repent from sin, pride, wrong attitudes, and unforgiveness. Keep a journal during your fast to write down your fasting goals and to record your prayer and fasting adventures with God.

3. **Remember to pray and read God's Word.** This may seem obvious, but fasting without prayer and meditating on the Word is . . . well . . . *dieting.* We fast to focus more completely on God.

4. **Fast by faith**. Often breakthroughs, needed direction, etc. come after fasting—sometimes much, much after. Don't let the enemy discourage you into thinking that your fast isn't accomplishing anything. Take any amount of opposition as encouragement to press on with all fervency. God rewards every fast done with godly intentions.

5. **Sustained personal revival and a fasted lifestyle go hand-in-hand.** Study revival history, and you'll be hard pressed to find revivalists who didn't incorporate seasons of fasting into their prayer lives. Almost every great move of God has been birthed in prayer and fasting. Living a fasted lifestyle is a must if you want to experience nonstop personal revival.

Questions
for
Reflection

→ What fasting challenges and victories have you experienced?

→ List reasons you have fasted in the past (or could now).

→ How can you intentionally live a fasted lifestyle?

Prayer for Personal Revival

Lord, I want to live a fasted lifestyle so that I'll always hunger for You.

Help me develop the spiritual discipline of fasting.

Show me the types and lengths of fasts You want me to undertake.

Help me to resist distractions and not get sidetracked.

I want my fasting to cultivate a greater intimacy with You.

Forgive me for the times I have craved food, or anything else,

more than You. I want You to be the passion of my heart, God.

Use fasting to help me draw closer to You in every way, every day—

and align my life to Your Word. As I fast, set my heart on fire for You

and allow me to experience personal revival.

I love you, Lord! In Jesus' name I pray.

Amen.

DAY 12

Thirsty to Hear God's Voice

JOHN 10:1–21

> **LOOK BACK**: Yesterday you were awakened to the spiritual discipline of fasting. Tell God of your willingness to fast in order to hunger and thirst more fully after Him. Ask Him how He would have you live a fasted lifestyle. Obey what He tells you and plan your fast accordingly.

"I can't hear God's voice."
"God speaks to so-and-so more than me."
"I ask God to speak to me, but He rarely does."

These are lies the enemy wants you to believe. The truth is this: God speaks to you. Actually, He talks to you—a lot. Are you listening?

I believe it isn't a lack of desire that stops many Christians from achieving intimacy with God. Most Christians would love to have a deep love relationship with Almighty God. No, often the hindrance is the perceived inability to hear His voice.

It's difficult to have a close relationship with someone when you do all the talking. Instead of a dialogue, your time spent together becomes a monologue. Two-way communication is at the heart of all intimate relationships.

The parable of the Good Shepherd and His sheep clearly presents the case that hearing the voice of God is a way of life for the Christian. Having ears to hear is normal Christianity. Jesus confirms this when He said: ". . . the sheep recognize His voice . . . they know His voice. . . . They will listen to My voice" (John 10:3–4, 16).

While there are many times I leave the place of prayer without hearing the voice of God, I always expect to. My expectation is so high that I never spend time with God without taking a notebook and pen. Interestingly, when I didn't expect Him to speak, I rarely heard His voice. But now that I expect it, I hear God speak with much more frequency—both in my devotional time as well as throughout my entire day.

God leads us by His voice, similar to the "I Spy" game we played as children. "I see something blue. You're warm, you're cold, you're getting warmer. . . ." God speaks one clue at a time, one dream at a time, one impression at a time. He doesn't usually give us the entire picture, but just enough for us to know the next step. In doing so, He's building our faith and deepening our trust in Him.

Some encounters with God's voice are more obvious than others, but eventually we realize He's been leading us all along. God's voice leads us even when we don't recognize it. For example, if you've ever heard yourself saying any of these things, you've heard the voice of God:

- I felt impressed to walk to a different part of the store and met someone who needed prayer.

- I was looking for a job and ran into someone who told me about a company that was hiring.

- That's strange. I dreamed about that very thing last night.

- I read my Bible and a Scripture leapt off the page.

- I'm going through the most difficult trial ever, but I have the peace that passes all understanding (Phil. 4:7).

God has as many ways to speak as there are grains of sand on the beach. He's creative and does things differently each time. Don't be fooled into thinking He will speak to you the same way He did the last time you were in the same situation. He won't; He will probably speak an entirely different way.

His voice could sound like an impression or a knowing in your "knower." He could speak through a dream, a vision, or through the wise counsel of another. He might communicate through a quickening of Scripture, a worship song that suddenly comes to mind, or an open or closed door.

There have been times in my life when the volume of God's voice was so loud I couldn't miss it if I tried. And other times I've had to really lean in and intently listen—like listening to what is being said in the next room. Shutting out distractions and keeping your heart free from anxiety, unforgiveness, and discouragement (which act like static on a radio) are necessary to hear God's voice regardless of the method He utilizes.

Some guardrails of confirmation that you've heard God's voice:

- It'll always line up with the Word of God. God will never ask you to do anything that contradicts His Word. In fact, the Bible is the primary way God speaks to His people.

- In the multitude of counselors there is safety. If unsure, ask those wiser in the Lord than you.

- A God idea will grow stronger; a good idea will wane.

- God's directives will always require faith and courage.

- When you step out in faith to do what God has spoken, check your spirit. Do you have peace or turmoil? Let the peace of God (or lack thereof) be your umpire.

- Did you do the last thing God told you to do? He's not going to give you a new instruction until you have obeyed the last one.

There is absolutely nothing in the entire world that compares to hearing the voice of Almighty God. One encounter with His voice can literally change your life forever. Let your Christian walk be revived by leaning into God's wondrous voice with eager anticipation.

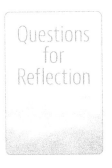

Questions
for
Reflection

→ How did God speak the first time you heard His voice?

→ Where do you hear God the clearest?

→ What changes can you make to tune your ear Wto God's voice more intently?

Prayer for Personal Revival

Lord, I'm Your sheep and You are my Shepherd.

I'm so grateful that You desire to speak and lead me by Your voice.

Help me to shut out all distractions and quiet the noise.

They drown out Your voice. Teach me to discern Your voice

from all other voices. There's nothing I want more than to have

an intimate relationship with You, which includes an ongoing dialogue.

Give me ears to hear Your voice every day, all day.

Help me quiet my thoughts and heart so I can hear You clearly.

I love You, Lord! In Jesus' name I pray.

Amen.

DAY 13
Thirsty for Worship

LUKE 7:36–50

> **LOOK BACK:** Yesterday you renewed your thirst to hear God's voice. In today's prayer time, write down anything you believe the Lord might be speaking. After running it through the confirmation guardrails, continue to pray it through until the Lord releases you to act on what you've heard.

Perhaps one of the most outstanding instances of worship in the New Testament is the story of the sinful woman who worshiped at the feet of Jesus (Luke 7:36–50). She epitomizes a true worshiper. Jesus was worshiped as she:

- knelt at His feet
- washed the dust from His feet with her tears
- dried His feet with her hair
- repeatedly kissed His feet
- anointed His feet with expensive perfume.

Notice some of the details glaringly absent from this scene:

- fog machines and synchronized light shows
- a finely tuned professional band
- me-centric "worship" songs
- production crews, scripts, and schedules

- a countdown clock to ensure worship doesn't last one second too long

- an upbeat song, followed by a medium-fast song, and then two really slow songs.

You get the point.

Lord, forgive us for what we've made worship!

Empty religion thrives on form. When worship is reduced to a formula it becomes lifeless and useless. But if worship is heartfelt, it reaches God's throne and touches His heart.

Worship is love and desire expressed. When we worship God, we lavish our profound love and deep desire for Him. The source of authentic worship is a burning heart and a passionate love relationship with Jesus. *Blessed be the name of the Lord!*

Worship is also a heart softener to prepare for personal revival. The fallow ground of our hearts must be broken in order for repentance to transpire and revival to take root. Worship is the match; our hearts are the altars. Worship births personal revival and personal revival births worship. They work harmoniously with each other in continuous motion.

A revived Christian is a true worshiper. Believers who have experienced personal revival live a lifestyle of worship. They freely worship in aisle six of the grocery store and behind the cubicle at work, as much as they do during a church service. The woman who was forgiven of much expressed her love, gratitude, and joy through the language of worship. She freely worshiped Jesus because Jesus had set her free.

Like the woman, on-fire Christians aren't dependent on music or hype to worship the King. Worship is who they are and what they do. They live to worship Jesus no matter where they are or what they're doing. They also don't care who's watching. From the woman's perspective, there was one person in that crowded room—Jesus.

Have you ever been asleep in a completely dark room when someone walks in and turns on the lights? "The light hurts my eyes!" you shout. "Turn it off!" Same thing happens when the spiritually lost or lukewarm observe a believer worshiping Jesus with reckless abandon. When we demonstratively worship Jesus, we'll always draw the ire of those who aren't.

Tell her to stop.

She's way over the top!

She just wasted that money on Jesus.

It should've gone to a better cause.

What's she doing?

Everyone knows her past.

She isn't kidding anyone.

True biblical worshipers give their all no matter the price. The woman worshiped Jesus with perfume that cost a year's wages. On top of that, the perfume container wasn't like today's bottles that dispense a little at a time. No, to get the perfume out, she had to break the jar (similar to an old piggy bank).

She knew she couldn't give just part of the perfume to Jesus. It was all or nothing. There was no hesitancy on her part. There was no, "Should I give God my all, or should I hold some back?" She didn't decide, "God, that part is yours, but this part over here, is mine."

Worshipers give themselves fully to the worship of their Savior, no matter how they appear to others. She didn't care what people thought. Jesus was the center of her attention. Worshipers don't allow the fear of man to have any part of their worship. If they do, they'll be tempted to "tone it way down."

Daily we choose to joyfully pour ourselves out on Jesus without limit or restraint. But when we lose sight of all Jesus has done for us, we start withholding our worship. There's no such thing as a closet Christian or a closet worshiper.

"But the time is coming—indeed it's here now—when true worshipers will worship the Father in spirit and in truth. The Father is looking for those who will worship him that way" (John 4:23).

Therefore, Christians who desire sustained personal revival 1) make worship a lifestyle, 2) worship Jesus with reckless abandon, 3) never forget what Jesus has done for them, and 4) give no place to the fear of man or the flesh.

I'm that woman. So are you.

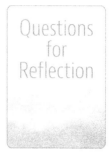

Questions for Reflection

→ Describe your present worship life.

→ What is your biggest struggle with worship?

→ Fast-forward five years. What's your worship life like?

Prayer for Personal Revival

Lord, I want to lavish my worship on You.

You deserve my worship when I'm on top of the mountain,

when I'm in the valley, and every day in-between.

Teach me to worship You the way You deserve to be worshiped.

Take me deeper in worship. Forgive me for holding back and for losing

sight of all You have done for me. Lord, revive my worship life.

I know that worship and personal revival go hand-in-hand.

I want to live a lifestyle of worship, never letting fear of man impede.

Today, I make the decision to freely express my love and desire for You in

the language of unhindered worship until I take my last breath.

I love You, Lord! In Jesus' name I pray.

Amen.

DAY 14

Thirsty for the Awe of God

LUKE 5:17–26

> **LOOK BACK:** Yesterday you were unleashed to freely worship God! Nothing again will stop you from demonstratively expressing your love for Jesus with reckless abandon. Start your time with the Lord by lavishing your unhindered worship on Him.

My husband and I sensed God directing us to move closer to our church, so we placed our home for sale. Unfortunately, the real estate market plummeted and our house value dropped by $20,000. We needed every penny in order to move. However, by faith, we began searching for a new home.

One morning, a few months later, the phone rang. The person calling identified himself as a Hollywood producer and writer; I thought it was a crank call. But he clarified that in addition to his work in Hollywood, he was also a Christian. He explained he wanted to purchase a domain name I owned for his personal ministry. He offered me $20,000. After much prayer, I joyfully accepted.

A few days later, he wired $20,000 into our checking account. That money, coupled with an offer we received to purchase our house, enabled us to buy our new home, located just eight minutes from church. This was the miracle my husband and I needed.

Oh, God, I'm in awe of You!

The awe of God is our response of wonder, reverence, and amazement at God's undeniable, active presence in our lives. It is a moment in time when we are overwhelmed by the awesome nature of God. The awe of God is when God's marvelous glory grabs our attention. The opposite of the awe of God is to view God and His ways as mundane or ordinary.

Jesus had just healed a paralyzed man who was lowered through the roof by his friends. It was an instant miracle; Jesus gave the command and immediately he was healed and walked home. The reaction of the crowd was captured in Luke 5:26: "Everyone was gripped with great wonder and awe, and they praised God, exclaiming, 'We have seen amazing things today!'"

When God moves powerfully, it's easy to be awestruck by Him. However, we also need to live in the awe of God on a daily basis—between the miracle—*now*. We need to experience the awe of God when we:

- recall the miracle of our salvation. The longer we're saved, the more awestruck we should be.

- receive fresh grace for an extremely difficult situation.

- have sinned and receive God's limitless mercy.

- open our Bibles and see the rich treasure it is, brimming over with gold, silver and precious gems.

- are enthralled that the God who created the heavens and the earth, loves us and wants to spend time with us.

- recognize that God's so much bigger than the problems we face.

- view God's beautiful handiwork and creation.

- reflect on Jesus' death on the cross—His glory, beauty, and love, as well as the dreadfulness of His suffering.

This list could go on forever.

While we understand that the world doesn't have an awe of God, let that not be said of us. The longer we follow the Lord, the more our awe should increase. Possessing an understanding of the awe of God is a significantly bigger deal than we can imagine. A lack of awe will affect our faith, joy, and relationship with God.

Here are three ways to recapture the awe of God:

1. **Childlikeness.**
   When we lose our awe, we stop living with childlike faith. My beautiful granddaughters, ages five and three, constantly remind me what this looks like. Things that seem mundane to me, they look at with wonder. Getting the mail, doing simple household chores, or helping me bake absolutely thrills them. Seeing life through the excitement in their eyes, helps revive the awe of God in my life. To recapture the awe of God, purposely view your relationship with God with childlike faith and wonder.

2. **Gratitude.**
   When we express our thankfulness to God, it shifts our focus from our list of problems to our big God. If we don't magnify the Lord through gratitude, God becomes small in our eyes and our problems appear huge. When we're grateful, it reminds us of the many things God has done for us, which serves to encourage our faith. To recapture the awe of God, intentionally incorporate thanksgiving into your daily devotions and express your gratefulness to Him all throughout your day.

3. **The Fear of the Lord.**
   I live near the Jersey shore. A multitude of t-shirt stores are on the boardwalk. One day as I "strolled the boards," a t-shirt hanging in the window caught my eye. It said: "Jesus is my homeboy." While I understand the message on the shirt (Jesus is our friend), it lacks the fear of the Lord. Without holy fear, we bring God down to our level and do not view Him with wonder. The reverential fear of the Lord leads to the awe of God, and the awe of God leads to the reverential fear of the Lord. To recapture the awe of God, we must possess a holy fear of the Lord.

→ What surprised you most from today's reading?

→ Have you lost your awe of God?

→ How can you become more childlike in your relationship with God?

Prayer for Personal Revival

Lord, I stand in awe of You!

Your greatness is beyond anything I can imagine or comprehend!

Help me live from a place of awe and wonder in every

facet of my life—the big things, as well as the ordinary.

Search my heart for anything that inhibits me from experiencing wonder.

Forgive me for the times I have brought You down to my level,

lost my awe of You, or viewed any part of my Christian walk as mundane.

Lord, restore my childlike faith, gratitude, and the fear of the Lord.

Though they don't realize it, the world is dying to increase in the awe of God.

Let them see me live in wonder.

I love You, Lord! In Jesus' name I pray.

Amen.

DAY 15

Thirsty for Soul Winning

LUKE 15

> **LOOK BACK:** Yesterday your awe and wonder of God was rekindled. Today, from a place of childlikeness, spend time telling God all the ways you are awestruck by Him. Take it one step further: share with someone one of the many aspects of God that amazes you.

The county fairgrounds were filled with people. Some had taken their families out for a day of fun in the July heat. Others were carnival workers selling food or operating rides. Still others were vendors selling their wares to make ends meet. Our church had a booth at the fair, offering prayer to every passerby.

For one week, from sunrise to midnight, we took turns manning the prayer station. We prayed for every imaginable felt need from "I'm suicidal" to "I need a job." We asked God to supernaturally intervene. The hearts of the people were warmed and open to hear the gospel after receiving prayer; God's presence encountered them. We presented the Truth to hundreds of people during that week and gave God the glory for using us in prayer evangelism.

One of the people who stood out among the rest was Mike. Mike was a Muslim who worked in a booth selling sunglasses and body-piercing jewelry. He wandered over to our tent after someone from our church handed him a gospel tract.

Mike had questions about the contents of the tract and explained that although he was thoroughly versed in the Koran, he knew very little about the Bible. He asked about the differences between Christianity and Islam. As one of our workers presented the life-changing gospel to him, I prayed for wisdom in choosing my words.

The Holy Spirit prompted me to say, "What is the biggest thing you need God to do for you? Think of something so big, so virtually impossible, that only a God who is alive and powerful could meet that need. Jesus wants to prove Himself strong to you!"

Mike got a perplexed look on his face. The concept that God cared deeply about his needs was completely foreign to him. Taking it one step further, it astounded him that we cared enough to sit in the scorching summer sun for an entire week, with sweat pouring down our faces as we pointed people to Jesus. Mike told us he would have think about what we asked and get back to us.

First thing the next morning, Mike found us and shared his personal prayer request. We asked Jesus to meet that need and reveal Himself as Lord and Savior. Although we never saw Mike again, we trust Jesus did just that.

See, you've never locked eyes with someone who is not deeply loved by Jesus. *But do we also love?*

Do we love people enough to make the Great Commission our first concern? Do we love the perishing enough to rescue them from burning flames? Are we willing to lay down comfort and fear to present the gospel boldly to everyone in our sphere of influence? Someone? Anyone?

When evangelism isn't a way of life for the Christian, it's a sign that we're in need of personal revival. When the unsaved people around us go virtually unrecognized as people in need of salvation, we've lost our passion for souls. Although personal revival will affect every aspect of our lives, its purpose remains clearly for the lost. When we're revived, it spurs us on to do what we should have been doing all along—evangelism.

Jesus tells three parables in a row in Luke 15: the lost sheep, the lost coin, and the lost son. These stories are in response to the complaints of the Pharisees and teachers of the law that Jesus was hanging out with tax collectors and notorious sinners.

The Pharisees viewed everyone through two lenses: the important and the unimportant. The important were, well—*them*. The unimportant were tax collectors, sinners, Gentiles, women, Samaritans, and *everyone else*. However, through these parables, Jesus sets them straight. In the parables of the lost sheep, the lost coin, and the lost son:

- Something of value was lost.

- When something of value went missing, an all-out search was conducted.

- There was great rejoicing when that valuable item was found.

Jesus was driving home these non-negotiable points:

- The lost matter to God.

- The lost should matter to us.

- Win the lost.

Jesus said, "And what do you benefit if you gain the whole world but lose your own soul? Is anything worth more than your soul?" (Matt. 16:26).

That means that one soul is more valuable than the combined wealth of the whole world.

One soul is beyond price.

   No suffering too severe,

      No laboring too hard,

         No trouble too great,

            No rejection too painful,

               No expense too large,

                  No fear too immense,

                     To win a soul for Christ.

<table>
<tr><td>

Questions
for
Reflection

</td><td>

→ Finish this sentence: my biggest struggle with evangelism is _____.

→ What has been your most memorable soul-winning encounter?

→ Read and meditate on Luke 15. What stands out the most?

</td></tr>
</table>

Prayer for Personal Revival

Lord, revive my passion for souls.

I admit that the Great Commission hasn't been a priority.

I ask You for an insatiable desire—one that'll never be satisfied—

to win the lost. I ask You for the holy boldness to proclaim the Truth.

Fill my day with divine appointments with the unsaved.

Open doors that man can't open. I ask You to help me present the

gospel with simplicity and clarity. Season my words with grace.

Help me to formulate my personal testimony so I can share with many

what You've done for me. Lord, fill my heart with Your love, so the lost may

see Jesus in me. I ask You for a vast harvest of souls.

I love You, Lord! In Jesus' name I pray.

Amen.

DAY 16

Thirsty to Make Disciples

MATTHEW 28:18–20

> **LOOK BACK:** Yesterday your passion for world evangelism was reignited. Today, while maintaining that passion, your thirst to disciple the one will be revived.

Few things come closer to capturing the heart of God than these words:

"Therefore, go and make disciples . . ." (Matt. 28:19).

Making disciples matters to God more than anything else in the entire world. God has entrusted us with what is most precious to Him—people.

Following Jesus means making disciples. Disciples make disciples. That's what they do and who they are. If you aren't a disciple of Christ, you can't make other disciples. But if you're His disciple, you're commanded to make disciples, who then make more disciples.

Wait, you mean ME?

I wouldn't know how to begin.

I'm not a teacher.

I wouldn't be able to answer all their questions.

I don't have the time.

People are messy. I don't want to get my hands dirty.

To all of those excuses (and the millions more the devil will help you formulate) I say:

We make disciples out of our love and obedience to God.

When my son was born, I didn't know anything about babies. I was an only child and had never been around children. I wondered, "How can I possibly be a good mother?"

Discharge day arrived. My beautiful new baby and I were going home. The maternity nurse came into my room with clipboard and pen. She rattled off questions from her "new mom" discharge checklist.

"Do you know how to change his diaper? Feed him? Burp him? Give him a bath?" My mind was swirling. My answers were, "No. No. No. No." The nurse must have seen the overwhelmed look on my face. (I think I tipped her off by asking if I had to set an alarm for feeding time, to which she answered, "Your baby is the alarm clock!")

The nurse gently set down her clipboard and calmed my concerns, "I can tell you love your baby. The most important thing to remember is that babies need love, and I can already tell you have that down. Everything else will come to you."

She was absolutely right. I loved him more than anything in the world. That love took care of everything else.

Our love for Christ and His people fuels the engine of disciple-making. It's because of love that we pour our time, the Word, prayer, fellowship, wisdom, encouragement, and correction into the lives of God's people. Love takes care of the details.

We also make disciples out of obedience. Simply put, Jesus tells us to do it—*so we do.* Obedience is the lifestyle of a disciple. We obey God instantly, even when it doesn't make sense or if it hurts. We obey Him when we don't see the benefit, when we don't feel qualified, or when it's inconvenient. We obey God completely and totally (partial obedience is disobedience). We make disciples.

And then we teach those we're discipling to obey God. When my relationship with Jesus was brand new, I endeavored to share with others whatever I learned about God and His Word. If my pastor preached on John

3:16, I found someone to explain John 3:16 to him or her. When I learned the basics of prayer, I invited several friends over to my home for a prayer meeting to impart what little I knew about prayer.

As I grew in my walk with the Lord, I cultivated intentional discipleship relationships. With the help of the Holy Spirit, I located people in my church to disciple. Weekly, we got together to study Scripture, pray, and worship. I invited them over for barbeques, attended Christian concerts with them, and made myself available by phone, in-between our weekly meetings.

I was so passionate about making disciples that I launched a discipleship ministry in my local church. With the permission of my pastor, I matched new believers with mature Christians, who also met weekly. At any given time, there were a dozen or more intentional discipleship relationships transpiring in our church. The fruit from that ministry continues to be exponential; I still hear reports of the long-term ramification of those discipleship relationships.

Jesus clearly modeled disciple-making. While His heart was for the masses, His strategy was to spend time with the few who would go into the world and make disciples. For three years He invested the majority of His time in His 12 disciples. Those 12 men turned the world upside with the gospel.

Are you ready to turn the world upside? Disciple one Christian to become a committed, fruitful, mature disciple of Christ.

A million candles can be lit from the flame of just one.

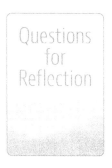

Questions for Reflection

→ Who has made the greatest impact on your Christian walk?

→ Who is someone in your life right now you can in turn pour into?

→ How does our love for Christ take care of the "how to disciple" details?

Prayer for Personal Revival

Lord, I want to obey the Great Commission.

I know that evangelism and discipleship are two sides to the same coin.

Revive my passion to make disciples just as You did for soul-winning.

Successful Christianity is having spiritual grandchildren.

Identify spiritual sons and daughters I can disciple

so they will, in turn, disciples others. Turning the world upside

with the gospel begins with pouring into the one.

Though I may not know how to disciple, I trust that

You will do it through me.

Help me to disciple others to look like You, Jesus.

May I spend my life making many disciples.

I love You, Lord! In Jesus' name I pray.

Amen.

DAY 17

Thirsty to Seek God's Face

2 CHRONICLES 7:14

> **LOOK BACK:** Yesterday God stirred your zeal to make disciples. Today, continue asking God to reveal those you can pour into. But don't let this day pass without imparting to someone a revelation you have learned from *Thirsty*. As you do, you'll begin to make disciples.

Eye color. Forehead expanse. Cheekbone placement. Nose size. Eyebrow thickness. Lip curvature. Face shape. These are the qualities that comprise a person's face.

But more important than a person's facial features, much more, is his or her countenance.

When I was a little girl, my mother would jokingly say, "Jamie, you could never play poker!" In essence, she was contrasting my inability to hide my facial expressions to the flat effect of a poker player hiding the hand he was dealt.

My mom was right. Absolutely everything shows up on my face. My facial expressions reveal when I'm pleased or frustrated, experiencing joy or sorrow, at peace or anxious, and content or seething with anger. Not only does the demeanor of my face display what I'm feeling, but it also divulges the strength and intensity of each of those emotions.

In addition to my inability to conceal my facial expressions, I have "a look." Actually, I have a bunch. There's my "mom look." It's that glance that communicates to my son everything from, "Say 'thank you' for that gift," to "You're in big trouble when we get home!"

I also have what's been coined "the Jim face." I inherited it from *Jim*, my dad. One of my granddaughters has it, too. "The Jim face" happens when I'm intensely focused on a task. I'm a person of many looks that convey a variety of messages.

God also has a face—a beautiful, magnificent face. His face is so alive that all other faces pale in comparison. And He has glances and looks. He radiates all He carries and who He is on His face. No, I'm not referring to the physical features of His face. I'm talking about what flows from His countenance: His glory, presence, and power.

One of the greatest passages on the study of revival is 2 Chronicles 7:14: "Then if my people who are called by my name will humble themselves and pray and seek my face and turn from their wicked ways, I will hear from heaven and will forgive their sins and restore their land." This Scripture outlines the basis and formula for true revival to occur. While many believers can quote this verse from memory, the phrase that many have difficulty understanding is:

". . . seek my face . . .".

Every believer should prioritize a place in his or her Christian walk of seeking the face of God. As a matter of fact, Christianity is the constant pursuit of His glorious face. While some of God's people have physically seen the face of God while on earth (just ask Jacob, Paul, and everyone in the four Gospels), we have the honor of seeking God's face by pursuing:

- **God's presence.** God's face and His presence are inextricably linked. Interesting to note, another name for the "Bread of the Presence" in the tabernacle was the "Bread of the Face." This freshly baked bread emitted an aroma that filled the tabernacle and beyond. It represented the presence of God to the people. Jesus, the Bread of Heaven, wants to release His presence to us, so that we, in turn, diffuse the fragrance of His presence to all. To seek God's face is to seek His presence.

- **God's purposes.** God is the ultimate Planner and has a wonderful, perfect plan. While we should seek God regarding His purposes for our individual lives, we also need to possess concern about God's overall plan. As a matter of fact, the latter should take preeminence in our prayer lives. To seek God's face means we press into both His plan for our personal lives, as well as His eternal purposes.

- **God's heart.** While our hearts are important to God, we make His heart our foremost concern. If God's heart is grieved, we allow our hearts to be penetrated with His grief. If something brings God joy, our hearts need to overflow with unbridled joy. Seeking God's face means we're honored and willing to live with the weight of God's heart pressing down on ours.

- **God's priorities.** When God gives us even a small glimpse of the burden of His heart, we turn that into intercession. Our prayers go from, "Bless me and mine," to "I cry out to You for the salvation of nations!" To seek God's face means that before we rattle off our laundry list of personal prayer needs, we ask Him for His prayer priorities.

- **God's perspective.** We're very good at viewing everything from our finite, how-this-affects-me perspective. As a matter of fact, we have made it an art form. God's perspective is the only perspective that matters—*always*. One look from God can change any long-held perspective we might possess. Seeking God's face means we lay aside our perspective and allow His eternal glance to change our view of particular person or situation.

- **God's favor.** Favor is more than just supernatural help to meet our felt needs. It means that I'm God's favorite. And you're God's favorite. Jesus loves us as much as the Father loves Him (John 15:9). His face is always turned toward us with unconditional love, joy, and delight. Seeking God's face means that we continually gaze at the One who has His face perpetually turned toward us.

May the fire we see in Jesus' eyes cause us to burn with passion for Him. May the look of love we see on Jesus' countenance radiate from our inmost being to the lost. May the glimpse of grief we see on Jesus' face, cut us—not like the hardly noticed discomfort of a paper cut—but like the deep pain of a surgeon's knife.

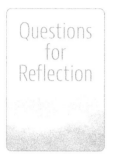

Questions for Reflection

→ What about today's reading gave you a different perspective?

→ Do you make the pursuit of God's face your lifelong pursuit?

→ How can gaining God's perspective change everything?

Prayer for Personal Revival

Lord, I want to see Your face.

As I gaze upon You, let me see Your glory, countenance, and power.

Let hardships and pain drive me to seek Your face.

Let the questions of life cause me to seek Your face.

Let weariness catapult me to seek Your face.

Let the temptations of the enemy cause me to seek Your face.

I want Your glory to permeate my entire being.

I want to impart Your fragrance to world.

Lord, I'm going to spend the rest of my days seeking Your face,

until the day I see You face-to-face.

I love You, Lord! In Jesus' name I pray.

Amen.

DAY 18

Thirsty to Die to Self

LUKE 9:21-27

LOOK BACK: Yesterday you learned what it means to seek God's face. Today, as you approach the place of prayer, press into His presence, purposes, and heart. Start by asking God to share His burdens and His perspective on every matter of your life.

"What area of your life does God want to crucify?"

This was the response of my pastor friend after I described the devastating betrayal I had just suffered.

"CRUCIFY?" I was looking for words of healing. I received the opposite.

I thought, "Was he listening when I relayed the painful betrayal details? Did he realize I had bruises on top of bruises? Did he misunderstand that a person I called 'friend' caused my heartbreak, *not God*! How could he possibly think that God wants to use this horrible betrayal to nail my flesh to the cross? He's wrong! *Or is he?*"

Our conversation continued. "Jamie, I know that every aspect of this betrayal has been utterly painful for you, but what part has been the most excruciating?" I stopped to think. In a flash, a specific episode popped in my mind. I conveyed to my friend the moment when it felt like a knife had plunged deep within my heart.

"That particular incident," he explained, "points to where you need to die to self." He ended our discussion by praying for the healing of my heart. He also prayed that I would allow God to use my Judas to make me more like Christ.

We hung up. My mind was reeling. I opened my Bible for solace. The Lord directed me to Luke 9:23: "If any of you wants to be my follower, you must give up your own way, take up your cross daily and follow me."

Ugh!

More than anything in the whole world, I wanted to follow Jesus. I wanted to follow Him so closely that the dust from His sandals was on my face. Still do. No, it was the rest of this verse that was troubling; the part where Jesus outlines the requirements for following Him:

". . . you must give up your own way, take up your cross. . . ."

What were Jesus' instructions for following Him? Allow Him to use every situation in your life to make you more like Christ. Run to the cross. Cling to God. Face the pain. Crucify the flesh. Choose obedience.

Fully dead to self equals fully alive in Christ.

I viewed this painful incident like a murder scene—carnage everywhere, nothing redeemable about it. But God's perspective was much different than mine (always is). The Potter wanted me to allow His loving hands to mold and shape me using this oh-so-painful event.

God changed my perspective using my pastor friend. I now viewed this ugly betrayal as an opportunity. A die-to-self classroom. An occasion to follow Jesus more closely. A moment in time to be grateful for every Judas God permitted to cross my path.

So instead of resisting the process of crucifixion through which God was taking me, *I yielded to it.* When my will opposes God's will, I have a decision: follow Jesus—or myself. God versus self.

Because here's the thing:

The opposite of the Kingdom of God is the kingdom of ME.

So, what might dying to self look like on an ordinary, run-of-the-mill, typical kind of day? Perhaps something like this:

- The Lord wants me to build relationships with my neighbors, but I would rather not. What if they give me the cold shoulder or, worse yet, have really messed-up lives and start telling me their problems? I choose *not* to die to self by pretending I don't notice them when I check the mail.

- My husband and I just had an argument and the Lord wants me to apologize. But what if he starts thinking of all the other times I've been wrong. I might lose credibility for future fights. Besides, he's hurt me before and didn't apologize. I choose *not* to die to self by saving face.

- My church is receiving a special offering and the Lord wants me to give. But I already gave my tithe in the regular offering. Besides, it would stretch my budget. I won't be able to buy my fancy macchiato before work each morning. I choose *not* die to self by ignoring the promptings of the Holy Spirit.

- My church is going door-to-door soul winning and the Lord wants me to go. It's the only day I get to sleep in and I really need my rest. Besides, slamming doors, snarling dogs, and rejection are not how I plan to spend my Saturday. I choose *not* to die to self by saying I have a previous commitment.

- The nursery needs help and the Lord wants me to volunteer. I know those babies need Jesus, but spending time changing diapers and singing stupid songs would make me *uncomfortable*. Besides, I would probably get scheduled to work in the nursery on a weekend I'm not available. I choose *not* to die to self by saying small children aren't my calling.

- I'm binge watching a TV series that I know God doesn't want me to view. I realize my eyes and ears shouldn't peer at the racy scenes peppered throughout, but a lot of Christians post on social media that it's their favorite show. Besides, I only tune in to decompress after a long day. I choose *not* to die to self by telling myself that I'm the exception to the rule.

The bottom line is this:

To follow Jesus means your flesh will suffer.
So be it. Obey anyway.

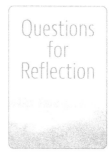
Questions
for
Reflection

→ What areas do you need to die to self?

→ Share a time you died to self and the blessing that ensued as a result.

→ Why is the opposite of the Kingdom of God the kingdom of me?

Prayer for Personal Revival

Lord, self-centered living stands diametrically opposed to Kingdom living.

I repent for every time I've lived to make myself happy,

instead of obeying You. I'll follow You at all cost, regardless of how I feel,

how uncomfortable it makes me, or how loud my flesh screams.

I choose to please You rather than gratify myself.

Uncover areas of my life where I must decrease, so You may increase.

My ultimate goal is to look more like You. From now on,

I'll view every circumstance in life as an opportunity to die to self, give up

my own way, take up my cross, and follow You—no matter how painful.

I love You, Lord! In Jesus' name I pray.

Amen.

DAY 19

Thirsty to Abide

JOHN 15:1–17

> **LOOK BACK:** Yesterday you received fresh revelation of the importance of dying to self. Take a moment to view every problem as an opportunity to crucify your flesh. Ask God to make you more like Christ, using people who cause you angst. Jesus is worth any amount of pain you endure!

Connect . . . Disconnect . . . Near . . . Far . . . Close . . . Distant . . . Up . . . Down . . . Around—and Around.

For many of us, this cycle describes our relationship with God. But this is not God's intention for the believer. He wants us to *abide* in Him, not have visits with Him, or shift in and out of His presence.

Jesus wants to be our home; the place we dwell. He wants us to come boldly to His throne and remain there. Jesus' blood gives us unhindered, unlimited access to the throne of God 24 hours a day, seven days a week. Therefore, we must learn to abide.

The parable of the True Vine, in John 15:1–17, illustrates the concept of abiding in Christ. The Gardener represents the Father, the True Vine is Jesus, and the branch symbolizes the believer. This parable presents a beautiful, intimate love relationship between Christ and the Christian. Abide (or some form of the word) is mentioned ten times in this passage.

To abide means to remain or stay. In human relationships, it takes both parties to stay connected. In our relationship with Christ, the only danger of disconnection remains on our part. Jesus will never disconnect from us, leave us, or forsake us. He is faithful and true. His love is unending, unconditional, and perfect.

While there are no formulas for how to abide (we all have different relationships with God), here are some thoughts to help you on your quest to learn how to abide in Christ:

- **Abiding in Christ isn't an option.** "Abide in Me" is a command, not a preference. We won't experience personal revival without it. The branch is created to attach to the vine; it's incomplete without it. When it's not attached, it's dead and becomes fireplace kindling. Don't believe me? Try living detached from Jesus for any length of time. *Dry. Lifeless. Fruitless. Exhausted.*

- **See Jesus as your source of life.** In order to abide, we must see our dire need. Jesus is our strength, wisdom, peace, love, and everything. While we can clearly see the beauty, blessings, and rest that abiding in Christ provides, we must also view it as a necessity.

- **Jesus will teach you how to abide.** The initial step to abiding is to ask Jesus to help you. Apart from Him we can do nothing—even abide. Jesus has been waiting to take you to the place of abiding. Tell Him of your desire. Abiding seems impossible, but Jesus makes the impossible possible.

- **Don't wait to abide until you understand it.** Perhaps you have been a Christian for a while, but abiding in Christ is new for you. Or you never really understood what it means. Just like with any biblical principle, don't wait to understand it before obeying. If we do, we'll never get around to doing it. Abide, by faith.

- **Start abiding now.** God gives us grace for each day. Today you have the grace to abide. And every day thereafter, you'll have the grace for that particular day to abide. Your daily decision to abide is like a link in a chain that forms a lifetime of abiding in Jesus. Each day, every moment of every day, turn your attention to Jesus.

- **The foundation of abiding is clutching God's Word.** Read it. Meditate on it. Memorize it. Believe it. Think it. Stand on it. Clutch the Word to your heart in times of question, confusion, and discouragement. Clutch the Word in times of decision, transition, and loneliness. The Word of God is your very life. Hold to it with everything in you.

- **Cling to Jesus like a child**. Picture a child clinging to his mother's leg, not letting go. Cling to Jesus with your thoughts, emotions, will, heart, love, worship, and prayer. The moment we stop clinging, we stop abiding. Children who cling less are growing up, but not so with the Christian. The *more* we cling to Jesus, the *greater* our maturity in the Lord.

- **Trust attaches us to Jesus.** Like a baby's umbilical cord attaches to the mother, trust in Jesus attaches us to Him. No matter the situation, how small or life-altering, trust Jesus. Never leave that place of trust. When you start to doubt, quickly say to yourself, "No, I'm going to trust Jesus, even with this." Trust is a choice. Abiding comes through simple faith, especially in times of trial. Allow crisis to be your school of abiding.

- **Focus on the Vine, not the branch.** It's easy to bypass God when our eyes are on ourselves. The difference between striving to abide versus abiding from a place of rest, is to focus on Jesus. Repent of "branch mentality." Jesus did the work; our job is to gaze on Him.

- **Study how Jesus relates to the Father.** This is how the newly saved 12 disciples learned what it means to abide in Christ. Jesus modeled it right before their eyes. The relationship between the Father and the Son serves as our ultimate guide to abiding. "I pray that they will all be one, just as you and I are one—as you are in me, Father, and I am in you" (John 17:21).

- **When you stop abiding, turn your attention back to Jesus.** In times of adversity, when you catch yourself gazing at your problems, turn your attention back to Jesus. And when the trial is over, continue to abide in Him. When you sin, immediately turn your attention back to Jesus in repentance. No condemnation. Just continue abiding.

Pursue abiding in Christ with reckless abandon. He will meet you at your point of desperation. In turn, He will join you to Him, one in spirit, and take you to a place of intimacy with Him like you never thought possible.

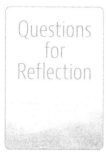

Questions for Reflection

→ How would you describe a roller-coaster Christian?

→ What lifestyle change do you need to make to abide in Christ?

→ Read and meditate on John 15:1–17. What spoke the loudest?

Prayer for Personal Revival

Lord, I know that the secret to maintaining personal revival

is abiding in Christ. When I continually abide in You,

I experience continual personal revival. Lord, teach me to abide.

From the time I open my eyes, until the time I lay

my head on the pillow at night, let me dwell in You.

Regardless of what life brings, help me to abide.

Use everything in my life, including victories and adversities,

to remind me to abide in You. When I've stopped abiding in You,

convict me so I can quickly turn my attention back to You.

Lord, I no longer want to move in and out of Your presence.

Therefore, I'm going to pursue abiding in You all the days of my life.

I love You, Lord! In Jesus' name I pray.

Amen.

DAY 20

Thirsty to Walk in Humility

JAMES 4:6–10

> **LOOK BACK:** Yesterday you determined to abide in Christ, all day, every day. No longer will you shift in and out of His presence. Today, when your quiet time with Jesus is over, stay connected to Jesus. Don't detach, no matter what the day brings. Cling to Jesus, clutch His Word, and practice His presence.

Pride.

Opposite of humility. Middle letter is "I." Gives glory to self. Trusts in self. Honors self. Is self-sufficient. Self-seeking. Blinds those who exhibit it. Creates an atmosphere where the enemy thrives. Won't go unpunished. God humbles those who possess it. God opposes people who have it. God hates it. The character of Satan. *Ugly.*

Humility.

Opposite of pride. God-focused. Gives glory to God. Trusts God. Honors God. God-reliant. Seeks God. Creates an atmosphere where God's Spirit moves. God exalts those who possess it. God gives grace to people who have it. God loves it. The character of Christ. *Beautiful.*

It's a daily battle to walk in Christ-like humility. Keeping our hearts free from pride is a struggle for all of us. And just when we think we've conquered pride (which is a form of pride), it creeps back unaware.

There's no getting around it: to experience personal revival, we need to eradicate pride—in every form—and walk humbly before our God.

While it's easy to spot pride in others, especially those who brag or think themselves higher than they ought, it's not so simple to recognize in us. Pride creeps in subtly, which is why we need to ask God daily to examine our hearts.

89

Here are some "pride detectors" to assist in recognizing the not-so-obvious areas of pride that may try to sneak into your heart:

- **Pride says**, "I know that already." **Humility says**, "I'll stay teachable, because there's always more to learn."

- **Pride says,** "I know I'm habitually late for meetings, but after all, they should be grateful I even go." **Humility says,** "It's not about my timetable, but when the meeting starts."

- **Pride says,** "I can't accept your gift. I'm a much better giver than receiver." **Humility says,** "Thank you for this blessing. I've learned to be a cheerful giver as well as a grateful receiver."

- **Pride says,** "I'm sorry to interrupt your conversation, but. . . ." **Humility says**, "I'll wait until you're finished talking. What you have to say is more important."

- **Pride says,** "I'm too embarrassed to invite that person over to my home. My carpeting is old and stained." **Humility says,** "That person's really hurting and needs the love of God. I'm going to invite him/her anyway."

- **Pride says,** "I refuse to be happy for their new car purchase. Can't they see that I've needed a new car for a long time?" **Humility says,** "I'm going to rejoice with them over this wonderful blessing. I know God will meet my needs as well."

- **Pride says,** "I always have to be in charge. It's just my personality." **Humility says**, "I don't have any problem with playing second-fiddle. I'll joyfully serve wherever needed."

- **Pride says,** "I can't believe they got the credit for that project! I'm the one who came up with that idea!" **Humility says,** "Let them receive the credit. I perform for an audience of One."

- **Pride says,** "I have difficulty publicly expressing my worship to God. I mean, what if someone thinks I'm weird?" **Humility says,** "I'm going to demonstratively worship God regardless of what anyone thinks. Worship is about God, not me."

- **Pride says,** "I'm lost in a strange city, but I'm not going to ask for directions." **Humility says,** "Let's pull over to that gas station. Saying, 'I don't know' is no problem for me."

- **Pride says,** "I'm so offended by what he said to me!" **Humility says,** "I refuse offense. People who are dead to themselves don't get offended."

- **Pride says,** "I'm visiting a church for the first time. I need to inform the pastor about all my ministry achievements and the initials behind my name." **Humility says,** "My gifts will make room for me—and promotion comes from the Lord. I'll never self-promote."

- **Pride says,** "I know I'm committing a sin, but God will understand because, well, after all, it's—*ME*." **Humility says,** "Even though everything in me desires to continue in that sin, I choose to repent. I'm not the exception to the rule."

- **Pride says,** "My pastor just corrected me. I'm going to look for a new church!" **Humility says,** "My pastor loves me and has my best interests at heart. Correction is necessary for my Christian growth. I'm willing to receive it and stay where God has planted me."

- **Pride says,** "I know I shouldn't skip my morning devotions, but my schedule is packed." **Humility says,** "I'm completely and totally dependent upon God. Prayerlessness is not an option."

→ Did you have any "ouch" moments from today's reading?

→ Were you surprised by any of the pride detectors?

→ Why do you think pride is easier to spot in others more than in yourself?

Prayer for Personal Revival

Lord, I acknowledge that I'm nothing, know nothing,

have nothing, and can do nothing without You.

My heart can't beat without You beating it;

I can't take another breath without You breathing into my lungs.

I'm utterly reliant upon You for absolutely everything.

Lord, search my heart for pride in any form.

Forgive me for prideful thoughts, deeds, and words.

From now on I choose to walk in Christ-like humility

in every area of my life.

Convict me if I'm ever tempted to operate in pride.

I love You, Lord! In Jesus' name I pray.

Amen.

DAY 21

Thirsty to Follow

MATTHEW 4:18–25

> **LOOK BACK:** Yesterday God revived your walk of Christ-like humility. As you go through your day, beware that pride will try to sneak back in. The moment it does, repent and walk humbly before God once again. There is nothing more beautiful than a Christian who displays humility of heart and complete reliance on Jesus for absolutely everything.

Peter and Andrew followed Jesus at once (Matt. 4:19).
James and John followed Jesus immediately (Matt. 4:22).
Large crowds followed Jesus wherever He went (Matt. 4:25).

The term "Christian" has become a very broad, catch-all term in our Western culture. To some, it means a churchgoer. To others, it refers to a person who is spiritual. And still to others, it's someone who believes there is a God. The true biblical meaning entails so much more, but here is a simple definition:

A Christian is someone who follows Christ.

I was given a trip to Israel for my 50th birthday. It was my first time to the Holy Land and I was elated. When my plane touched down in Israel, I determined to learn as much as possible. If you've ever toured Israel, you understand there is a tremendous amount to absorb. It's like drinking from a fire hose. But by far, my greatest lesson was this: I learned what it looks like for a disciple to follow.

One of the scenes you observe when you visit Israel are clusters of orthodox rabbis with their young disciples. These boys emulate their rabbi in every way. They literally follow his every move.

As the rabbi walks through the streets of Jerusalem, his disciple scurries closely after him. The boy sits where he sits, eats what he eats, sleeps where he sleeps, talks like he talks, and believes what he believes. The disciple forsakes all to follow his rabbi. When the boy becomes distracted and isn't following as closely as he should, the rabbi gives him correction. In response, the young disciple quickly adjusts himself and starts following once again.

When Jesus asked His disciples to follow Him, He was speaking to first-century Jews. They also had the same "what it looks like to follow" picture in mind. Knowing what it entailed, they followed him, *at once, immediately*, and *wherever He went*. What a beautiful example of following Jesus!

In order to experience personal revival, we must ask ourselves these questions:

- *Am I following Jesus?*
- *Are there areas of my life I'm not following Jesus?*
- *Am I following Jesus as closely as I should?*
- *Have I become distracted, in any way, from following Jesus?*

To help answer these questions, I have boiled "following" down to four elements. While following Jesus is multi-faceted, I believe the simplicity of these foundational principles will help you view following Jesus with greater clarity.

To follow Jesus, we must:

- **Look at Jesus.** When I was a kid, I played "Follow the Leader." The objective of the game: give the leader your full attention in order to mimic his or her actions. If I got distracted and took my eyes off the leader, I lost the game. Same with following Jesus.

    We can't follow Jesus unless we keep our eyes fixed on Him. If we look at our circumstances, problems, people, or even ourselves, we'll have great difficulty following Jesus. To continually follow Him, we need to keep our eyes on Him.

- **Walk behind Jesus.** To successfully follow, we can't walk in front of Jesus, or even next to Him. We must walk behind. He leads, we follow. We follow Him, He's not following us. When we live according to our own agenda, we walk in front of Jesus.

In Matthew 16:23, Jesus told Peter to get behind him when Peter voiced his objection to Jesus' death on the cross. When we place our will above God's, we're walking in front of Him. When we mix His will with our will, we're walking beside Him. No, to fully submit to God's plans for our lives and to stay in step with His Spirit, we must follow closely behind— and stay behind.

- **Love Jesus.** "You must love the LORD your God with all your heart, all your soul, and all your mind" (Matt. 22:37). In this first and greatest commandment, Jesus makes it clear: followers of Christ love Him with everything in them, which includes the good times and bad. Sadly, however, some won't.

  Jesus had just taught a hard message. "Unfollowing" Jesus was the response of a group of His disciples. "At this point many of His disciples turned away and deserted Him" (John 6:66). The love of Christ must compel us to follow Him no matter what.

- **Obey Jesus.** Jesus said, "If you love me, obey my command-ments" (John 14:15). Obedience *to* Jesus is the evidence of our love *for* Jesus. We obey whether we feel like it or not. Not the "I'm going to count to ten and you better do what I say, 1 . . . 2 . . . 3 . . ." kind of obedience. No, as followers of Christ we obey completely and instantly, even when everything within us wants to disobey or delay God's directives.

Do you love Jesus enough to still follow Him when things get difficult? What if He leads you to a really hard place? Is your "following" conditional?

What if it means sacrifice, pain, grief, question, disappointment—and even persecution?

Will you still follow Jesus if He asks for that level of obedience?
He is.

Questions
for
Reflection

→ How closely are you following Jesus?

→ Have you ever "unfollowed" Jesus (even in your heart)?

→ Is your following Jesus conditional based on where He leads?

Prayer for Personal Revival

Lord, help me to follow You more closely than I ever have

in my Christian walk. I want to follow Your every move from a heart of

submission, love, and obedience. Root out any rebellion from my heart.

Any time my eyes are fixed on something or someone else,

remind me to place them squarely back on You.

Help me to always walk behind You, and never in front or beside.

Help me to love You more—even during times of hardship.

Lord, I want to obey You instantly, completely, and at all cost.

Help me to obey Your Word, Your will, and Your way. Search my heart,

Lord, for anything that hinders from following hard after You.

I love You, Lord! In Jesus' name I pray.

Amen.

DAY 22

Thirsty for the Blessings of Brokenness

PSALM 51

> **LOOK BACK:** Yesterday you determined to follow Jesus no matter the difficulty, pain, or trial. Tell Him, once again, you will follow wherever He leads. As the day unfolds, keep your eyes on Jesus, walk behind Him, love Him, and obey Him.

Chip. Chip. Chip. Chip. Chip . . .

Sculptors create masterpieces one chip at a time. With a hammer, chisel, and block of marble, they begin the seemingly endless chipping process with an end goal in mind—for example, a person's face. They chip away everything that isn't that person. And they don't stop chipping until the marble bears the image of that person.

Our highest purpose in life is to reflect the image of Jesus. Therefore, the Lord chips away everything that isn't of Him. God needs to break off of Jamie Morgan all that isn't Jesus. And I need to cooperate with the chipping.

God isn't looking for perfect vessels, but broken vessels. As followers of Christ, we must allow the Lord to break us. He wants to shatter everything that isn't Jesus, in order to put us back together again—to look like His Son. And, more often than not, God uses suffering to do it. Friend, you may not want to hear this, but it's crucial you understand that:

Suffering is part of the Christian walk.

A few years ago, I interviewed 22 pastors for a dissertation I was writing on the topic of revival. Each of these pastors experienced a mighty outpouring of God's Spirit at some point during his or her ministry and was eager to share how God had moved in his or her church.

After conducting all the interviews, I carefully reviewed the transcripts and made a fascinating discovery: right before revival broke forth in these ministries, every one of them had experienced some sort of brokenness.

The types of suffering the pastors experienced varied from minister to minister. But they included things like betrayal, grief, a prodigal child, personal failure, setbacks, unexpected hardships, rejection of some sort, or a season of criticism. Bottom line: they experienced some sort of intense pain. Did God cause these things to happen? Absolutely not. But if we can learn anything from the Book of Job it is this: nothing can touch us without first passing through the hands of God.

God allows us to go through trials in order to do a deep, preparatory work in our lives. He turns around for good what the enemy means for harm. God brings us to a state of brokenness so He can pour His Spirit into empty vessels. He needs to be able to trust us with His fire. We need to become weak in ourselves so we can operate in the strength and power of God.

Recently, I happened upon this entry in my prayer journal. I penned it during a season of brokenness in my life:

> I'm in pain and wandering the wilderness; the pain is more agonizing than I can bear. I can't seem to find my way out. I have a broken heart and my bruises have bruises. This has affected my life in ways most will never know or understand. There have been many times in my life when I felt like my head was just barely above water; this time I feel like I'm drowning with only seconds left to live.

Although this period of my life was excruciatingly painful and something I never want to experience again, there was purpose in the pain. Somewhere during this season of suffering, my focus shifted. Instead of staring straight at the pain of my throbbing heart, I lifted my eyes to see the loving hands of the Sculptor at work in my life. I came to the realization that what God allowed me to endure was for my highest good. And right in the middle of brokenness, I experienced unspeakable joy. I now know God in ways I wouldn't otherwise.

There are things that God accomplishes in our brokenness that can't be achieved by other means. Brokenness is essential for our spiritual maturity. It is critical for maximum usefulness by the Master. David learned that God is drawn to our brokenness.

In Psalm 51:16–17, David told the Lord, "You do not desire a sacrifice, or I would offer one. You do not want a burnt offering. The sacrifice you desire is a broken spirit. You will not reject a broken and repentant heart, O God." When our hearts are broken before God, He becomes our *everything*. God loves our brokenness. Our brokenness is beautiful before the Lord.

A few thoughts about the process of brokenness:

- **First, it's slow.** Just when you think the Sculptor is finished chipping away, He's not. When you surmise an aspect of your life is fine and that it's time to move on to another area, God finds yet something else to chisel. Warning: during the process of chipping, chipping, and more chipping, there will be a temptation to quit. Give the Artist all the time He needs. He knows exactly what He is doing.

- **Second, don't doubt the goodness of God.** Often during the process of brokenness, the enemy will tempt you to question God's goodness. Where is God? Did God fail you? Does God really have a future for your life? When will this trial be over? Did God forget you? All of Satan's strategies are designed to destroy your faith. The enemy knows if he can get you to doubt God's goodness, you'll drop your shield of faith. Your response needs to be, "I'll suffer my whole life if I have to. I've found God in my brokenness and He is all I need."

- **Third, the greater the calling, the greater the carving.** It's true. Big purpose equals big preparation. The person with an unbroken spirit will never experience his or her true potential in God. During the process of brokenness, you'll learn lessons: it's not man's applause, recognition, or approval I need; I live only to please God. You will become so deeply rooted in Him that no matter what the storm, you'll not be moved. If you're willing to let the Master do His work, He will enable you to stand through any type of adversity.

The steps to becoming God's masterpiece are joyful, painful, and necessary for you to reflect the glory of His Son. Suffering is always involved. Few are willing to pay the price. But God reaches into the depths of the hearts of those who do and says, "I love you. I'll restore you. I'll use you."

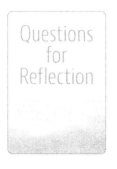

Questions for Reflection

→ Meditate on Psalm 51. What is God saying to you through this passage?

→ Describe a season of brokenness in your life.

→ Have you ever resisted the chiseling of God?

Prayer for Personal Revival

God, I choose to see Your hand in every situation of my life.
Break me, Lord. Chip away everything that isn't Your Son.
Break my unbendable will, unruly emotions, and determined mind.
Break my flesh that screams for everything it shouldn't have.
Break my unyielding, hardened heart. Break me of self-love,
self-reliance, and self-sufficiency. Break me of pride and fear.
Break me of my opinions, my ways, and my plan.
I'll not shrink back from suffering, but am willing to pay any price
to pursue the high calling and destiny you've purposed for my life.
Lord, I offer myself, without reservation, into Your loving hands.
I love You, Lord! In Jesus' name I pray.
Amen.

DAY 23

Thirsty for Freedom

JOHN 11:1–44

LOOK BACK: Yesterday you yielded to the Sculptor's chiseling. You asked God to break your will, unruly emotions, and flesh. You submitted to the breaking of your hardened heart, pride, and self. Today, don't shrink back from any amount of suffering or brokenness required. Resembling Jesus is the Christian's ultimate goal.

Observation from my 32-year Christian journey: it is impossible to mature spiritually while possessing an unhealthy soul.

I've seen it over and over again. A Christian who wants more than anything to grow, hits a ceiling of emotional woundedness (which affects every issue of life). Personal revival is difficult to sustain when we're bound in any area of our life.

Why? Our graveclothes cause us to trip.

Lazarus was terminally ill. His sisters summoned Jesus to pray for him. In the interim, Lazarus died. His sisters thought all hope was lost. But with Jesus there is always hope and His timing is always perfect!

When Jesus arrived on the scene, Lazarus had been dead for a few days. "Then Jesus shouted, 'Lazarus, come out!' And the dead man came out, his hands and feet bound in graveclothes, his face wrapped in a headcloth. Jesus told them, 'Unwrap him and let him go!'" (John 11:43–44).

Graveclothes represent the life we lived before we were born again.

The moment we receive salvation, we're brand-new creatures in Christ Jesus. Our spirit, which was once dead, comes alive. But our soul (mind, will, and emotions) remains unchanged and in desperate need of an encounter with God. Therefore, our graveclothes must be removed.

Graveclothes often reveal and expose:

- lies embraced
- truth to apply
- wisdom to employ
- spiritual disciplines to incorporate
- destructive habits to surrender
- sins from which to repent
- strongholds to break
- pain to heal
- priorities to be adjusted
- growth to transpire.

While there are probably multiple areas of our lives where graveclothes need to be removed, God usually works on one or two at a time. For this reason, it is important to determine the specific aspects of our lives where we can sense the activity of God at work.

To assist in identifying these areas, here are ten "Ms" that represent the parts that comprise the whole of our lives. Invite the Holy Spirit to highlight how He is lovingly removing your graveclothes:

Here are the ten "Ms":

1. **Master**: How is your relationship with God? Devotions? Bible reading? Prayer? Fasting? Worship? Personal Retreats? Sabbath keeping? Faith? Unbelief? Obedience? Rebellion? Habitual sin? Generational iniquity? Addiction?

2. **Mind**: How is your thought life? Meditate on the Word? What are you thinking? Toxic thoughts? Casting down negative imaginations? Unclean thoughts? Guarding your eye and ear gates? Fear? Guilt? Shame? Discouragement? Mental strongholds? Damaged emotions?

3. **Might**: How is the health of your physical body? Taking care of your temple? Nutrition? Exercise? Sleep? Rest? Balance? Physical strength? Routine medical exams? Stress level? Relationship to food?

4. **Motives:** What are the motives of your heart? Love? Good? Wrong? Impure? Vengeful? Selfish? People pleasing? Hidden? Selfish?

5. **Mouth:** What are you speaking? The Word? Encouragement? Uplifting? Negative? Idle? Careless? Gossip? Complain? Judgmental? Pleasing to God? Soft answers? Harsh? Vile language? Controlling your tongue?

6. **Money:** How are your finances? Tithe? Give offerings? Generous? Stingy? Good steward? Money your god? Spending addiction? Bright, shiny object syndrome? Store treasures on earth? In heaven? Trust God for provision? Work hard?

7. **Ministry:** What is God doing through you to reach the world? Obey the Great Commission? Walking in your calling? Freely give your testimony? Reach the hurting? Disciple the saved? Eternal perspective?

8. **Message:** What is the message of your life? Does it bring people closer to Jesus? Farther away? When people are standing at your funeral, how do you want to be remembered? Actions line up with your life's purpose?

9. **Mate:** How is your marriage? How is your singleness? How are the other relationships in your life? Toxic friendships? Ungodly associations? Are you trying to derive from them what can only be received from Jesus? What would they say about you?

10. **Minutes:** How do you spend your life? Good time manager? Waste time? Priorities in order? Make every day count? Guard time with God? Habitually late? Decisions about time reflect purpose? Maintain God's eternal perspective?

God will remove your graveclothes, but He usually does it with the assistance of the Body of Christ (like He did with Lazarus). Make an appointment with your pastor to receive wise counsel. Share your desire for unhealthy areas of your life to begin to flourish. Follow the advice of your pastor, and watch your graveclothes begin to fall off—one by one.

→ Do you detect graveclothes in your life?

→ How do they affect you?

→ What plans can you put in place to remove them?

Prayer for Personal Revival

Lord, I don't want anything in my life to hinder personal revival.

Shine Your Holy Spirit flashlight on any graveclothes hanging off my life.

The stench of death is trying to trip me.

I want my spirit, soul, and body to be healthy before You.

Help me cooperate with Your growth plan for my life.

Take the blinders off my eyes so I can see where I need to grow,

repent, and adjust. Identify unhealthy habits, unrepentant sin,

toxic emotions, ungodly relationships, wrong mindsets,

and anything else that thwart my love relationship with You.

I want freedom in every area of my life.

Thank you for calling me out of darkness into Your glorious light.

I love You, Lord! In Jesus' name I pray.

Amen.

DAY 24

Thirsty for the Presence of God

EXODUS 33:12–23

LOOK BACK: Yesterday you asked God to remove your graveclothes. Decide you won't let anything hinder your relationship with Him. Today, cooperate with the area of your life you sense the activity of God at work.

What marks you as a Christian?

Is it your Christian jewelry, your inspirational social media posts, or the bumper sticker on your car? Is it the size of your ministry, the vast Christian library you've accumulated, or the name of the church you attend? A conversation between Moses and God provides the answer to what sets a Christian apart from the rest of the world.

God directed Moses to lead the Israelites into the Promised Land. This was a huge assignment to say the least. Moses expressed he couldn't move forward without God: "For your presence among us sets your people and me apart from all other people on the earth" (Ex. 33:16).

The distinguishing mark of the believer is the presence of God.

It's important to note that Moses wasn't requesting something of God he'd never before experienced. Moses had personally encountered the manifest presence of God at the burning bush, the crossing of the Red Sea, and in the various wilderness miracles. Moses was simply asking God to do it once again.

There is a difference between God's omnipresence and His manifest presence. God's Spirit is everywhere, all the time. This is God's omnipresence. If you travel to the remotest part of Siberia and lift up a rock, God is there. If you venture to Zambia and ruffle the fur of a yak (do yaks have fur?), God's presence is under each hair. Wave your hand in front of your face. You just ran your fingers through the omnipresence of God.

God manifests His presence when He tangibly reveals Himself to our five physical senses. Paul's Damascus road encounter is an example (Acts 9:1–9). Paul saw a light from heaven (sight). The power of God caused him to fall to the ground (touch). And he heard the voice of Jesus (hearing). God's manifest presence affected three of Paul's five natural senses.

The story of Scripture begins and ends with God's manifest presence. God manifested Himself to Abraham as a smoking firepot and blazing torch, to Moses as a burning bush, and to the three Hebrews boys as the fourth person in a fiery furnace. In addition, God revealed Himself by the fire and smoke on Mt. Sinai, the wind that split the Red Sea, and the pillar of cloud by day and fire by night over the tabernacle. His presence could also be seen at the temple dedication as fire, as well as dew on Gideon's fleece.

In the New Testament God manifested His presence as a dove at Jesus' baptism, by tongues of fire and the sound of rushing wind in the Upper Room, and by the Lord suddenly transporting Philip away. Other biblical manifestations of God's presence included any time God's audible voice was heard (throughout the Bible), every sign, wonder, healing, miracle, and gift of the Holy Spirit in operation, and—*JESUS.*

Jesus remains the ultimate manifest presence of God.

I became a Christian two years before my husband Kurt. I did everything a good Christian wife does to lead my husband to the Lord. I prayed, scattered tracts around the house, and even anointed his pillow with oil. Kurt was an avowed atheist and wanted nothing to do with God. He also refused my many invitations to church. But an encounter with God's manifest presence changed everything.

One Wednesday night I invited Kurt to church. We were learning what the Bible says about marriage. I never thought Kurt would accept my invitation, but he did. Our marriage was in trouble and he was open to any help he could get.

As we walked through the door of the church that night, I said to

Kurt, "At the end of the class they pray for anyone in need. Why don't you ask them to pray for your knee?" Kurt had damaged his knee and was scheduled for knee surgery. I can still picture him hobbling up the church steps that night in terrible pain. He mumbled something under his breath, leading me to think he heard me but wasn't going to comply.

Near the end of the Bible study, the leader asked who needed prayer. Kurt reluctantly slipped his hand in the air and asked for prayer for his damaged knee. As the men gathered around Kurt and prayed, his knee began to visibly shake. Kurt's knee was instantly healed! When we arrived home from church that night, Kurt gave his life to Jesus. One encounter with the presence of God changed his life forever!

Revival transpires when God pours out His presence upon His people. First is God's presence, then revival—in that order. It is His presence that revives us. Experiencing God's presence is normal Christianity. When that isn't happening, we're in need of personal revival.

You may be thinking, "I don't know if I've ever experienced the manifest presence of God." In answer, I pose these questions to you: Have you ever had the "peace that passes all understanding" during a trial? How about joy unspeakable in a situation that was less than jubilant? Have you ever felt the conviction of the Holy Spirit? These are all manifestations of God's presence.

God wants to assure you that He is always present in your life. He loves to reveal Himself to you. Our job is to possess an unquenchable thirst for His presence. If you're not thirsty for God's presence, ask Him to make you thirsty. Determine to spend all the days of your life fulfilling your highest calling: pursuing the presence of God.

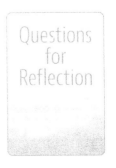

Questions for Reflection

→ Have you ever experienced the manifest presence of God?

→ Describe a time you experienced the peace that passes all understanding.

→ How can you become more aware of God's presence in your daily life?

Prayer for Personal Revival

Lord, just like Moses couldn't do what You asked of him

without Your presence, neither can I. Show me Your glory.

Make me thirsty for Your presence.

I invite Your presence into every part of my life.

Teach me how to become more aware of Your presence in my daily routine.

Help me carry Your presence everywhere I go.

I want Your presence to be evident to all.

Just as You encountered Paul on the road to Damascus,

encounter me however I need to be encountered.

Lord, I know that more knowledge, conferences, and even sermons

won't transform me. I'm only revived by Your presence.

The distinguishing mark of the Christian is the presence of God.

Lord, I want this to be a reality in my life.

I love You, Lord! In Jesus' name I pray.

Amen.

DAY 25

Thirsty to Persevere

JAMES 1:2-4

LOOK BACK: Yesterday God revived your thirst for His presence. Today, ask Him to give you greater sensitivity and awareness of His presence. Tell Him you want to be marked by and carry His presence all throughout your day, everywhere you go.

Every Christian has a perseverance threshold. What's yours?

Our threshold of perseverance determines the limit to which we're willing to push through the trials of life. It represents how long we'll continue steadfast in times of difficulty. It is the level we're willing to pursue Almighty God when the hordes of hell attack us at every turn.

A low perseverance threshold places perimeters around our Christian walk, including whether personal revival will transpire. Even if we experience revival, a low perseverance threshold affects the length of time it'll be sustained. If we don't cultivate perseverance, at some point we won't continue to:

- thirst after God
- pray without ceasing
- contend for revival
- press into God when things get hard
- allow the fire of adversity to change us into the image of Christ
- endure persecution for following hard after Jesus
- radically pursue Christ with everything in us.

If we draw a line in the sand and say, "No more!" we place a cap on how revived we could have been; our passion for God will be stymied. But a high perseverance threshold removes all limits from our pursuit of God.

But perseverance isn't just forging ahead, bearing under, or putting up with opposition of every kind. It's also about the attitude you have while you endure. James 1:2–4 gives us this key:

> Dear brothers and sisters, when troubles of any kind come your way, consider it an opportunity for great joy. For you know that when your faith is tested, your endurance has a chance to grow. So let it grow, for when your endurance is fully developed, you will be perfect and complete, needing nothing.

When James penned this epistle, Christians were experiencing intense persecution—the kind of persecution most of us will never understand. He admonished them to persevere, no matter how difficult their circumstances. Regardless of the pressure, stress, or ordeal, they were to stand their ground with unflinching faith and joy.

Faith, coupled with persistence and bolstered by joy, is everything we need to have victory in adversity.

Every unfavorable situation in life presents an opportunity to increase our threshold of perseverance. We grow in perseverance when everything in us screams not to persevere, but we persevere anyway. For example, I've grown in perseverance when:

- I battled Lyme disease for 15 long years, yet learned to joyfully possess an unwavering confidence in God's Word.

- God placed me in a job I didn't like (understatement), and I learned to joyfully stand, fixed and immovable, in God's perfect will.

- The host of the women's retreat where I had been asked to speak forgot to tell me the retreat was cancelled, and I learned to keep my eyes joyfully fixed on Jesus and forgive.

- I received correction from my pastor and I learned joyfully to not take offense because I knew it was pertinent for my Christian growth.

- I was persecuted by my brother-in-law for my devotion to Christ and learned to joyfully consider it an honor to share in the sufferings of Christ.

- I experienced three betrayals in one year by those I called "friends" and learned to joyfully allow God to use it to make me more like Jesus.

- I was falsely accused of something I didn't do, and learned to joyfully stay silent and allow God to be my Defender.

Each of these circumstances presented an opportunity for me to say, "I quit!" Instead, because I learned to endure, my perseverance threshold enlarged.

God doesn't waste pain!

Determine today that Jesus is worth any amount of pain you must endure to be everything for Him. No cost is too great in your hot pursuit of Jesus.

There is purpose in the pain of perseverance.

If you don't quit, you win!

Questions for Reflection

→ From 1–10, how would you classify your perseverance threshold?

→ What changes can you make to bring that number up to 10?

→ Describe a situation God used to grow your perseverance.

Prayer for Personal Revival

Lord, I don't want my present perseverance threshold

to hinder my level of personal revival.

Increase my threshold of perseverance.

Remind me to see every adversity in life as an

opportunity to grow in perseverance. Give me Holy Spirit resilience.

Help me to persevere as I'm stretched, taken out of my comfort zone,

and given needed correction. Remind me to persevere through

the pain of rejection, the ache of forgiving someone

who has done me wrong, and the sting of persecution.

Lord, help me to keep my eyes stayed on You

and take all limits off my perseverance threshold.

I love You, Lord! In Jesus' name I pray.

Amen.

DAY 26

Thirsty to be God's Friend

ROMANS 5:6–11

> **LOOK BACK:** Yesterday God increased your perseverance threshold and awakened your Holy Spirit resilience. Today, see every trial as an opportunity to walk by faith, maintain your joy, and grow in the fruit of perseverance. God doesn't waste pain, and neither should you.

Close friends are rare. I think most of us can count on one hand the people who fit the bill over our lifetime. Friendships usually take various other forms such as:

- **Acquaintances**. These are people who know of you, and you know of them, but there is no real relationship.

- **Casual Friends**. These friends are more surface, maybe even guarded. You never share the deep things of the heart.

- **Fair-weather Friends**. These friends only come around you when they have a need. And when you have one, they prove unreliable.

- **Good Company Friends.** These are friends with whom you enjoy each other's company because you have something in common. But the friendship drifts when your mutual interest halts.

- **Phone-a-friends.** These are your resource friends in time of need. They gladly make themselves available to you for needed direction, emotional support, and help of just about any kind. But it is understood that the relationship is one-way; when they need something, they know to look to elsewhere. In this type of friendship, you become the fair-weather friend.

And, last, the difficult-to-find intimate friend . . .

- **Intimate friends**. These people are friends during the good times and bad. They care deeply about you. They trust their hearts with you. They put your needs before their own. They are loving, patient, and generous. They simply can't spend enough time with you. *And*—you are all these things to them.

Friendship with God is reciprocal, not one-sided, fair-weather, or casual. It's wonderful that God calls me friend, but am I *His* friend? This question bears asking because personal revival is birthed from a place of intimate friendship with God.

The good news is that God yearns for friendship with you. As a matter of fact, He sent Jesus to die on a cross and shed His blood to have intimate friendship with you.

> For since our friendship with God was restored by the death of his Son while we were still His enemies, we will certainly be saved through the life of his Son. So now we can rejoice in our wonderful new relationship with God because our Lord Jesus Christ has made us friends of God (Rom. 5:10–11).

I became an intimate friend of God during a season in my life when all earthly friendships dried up. For a variety of reasons, friendships that were at one time soul-nourishing and life-giving were now either non-existent or distant at best. While we shouldn't wait for this to transpire, or even want this to occur (God wants us to have godly friendships), this is what happened to me.

Right in the middle of loneliness and pain, God drew me close to His side and invited me to partake in a level of intimacy I never dreamed possible. What I previously derived from my former circle of friends, I now received from God. But more important, the time, energy, love, care, and concern that I poured into those friendships, I now devoted to God. I found intimacy with God when I stopped looking to human relationships to fill a thirst that only He could quench.

I am a friend of God.

So what are some of the hallmark qualities needed to be God's friend?

1. **Loyalty**.

   Some believers just date Jesus. Oh, they love that He is a part of their lives; they can't imagine life without Him. But He isn't the center. He's more like an accessory, like a designer handbag or fancy baseball cap. They enjoy the benefits of dating Jesus, but without the commitment. In order to be a friend of God, we need to be loyal to God through thick and thin, by His side no matter what, and committed in our love and worship. Fickle and loyal can't coexist in our relationship with Almighty God.

2. **Transparency**.

   In order to have intimate, genuine, and authentic friendship with God, transparency is required. God calls every believer His friend, yet not all are willing to open their hearts to Him. God gives every Christian favor to access the deep places of His heart, but most will choose not to enter those deep realms. When we are friends with God, we express ourselves to Him without inhibition, and allow Him to do the same with us. It's impossible to have intimacy with God without transparency.

3. **Selflessness**.

   Preferring the other person over myself is an essential ingredient in any successful relationship. This also applies to our friendship with God. When I meet with God in prayer, do I give Him the opportunity to share His heart before I share mine? Do I place God's desires higher on my priority list than my own? Is pleasing God my sole longing, or do I want to please myself? Selfishness has no place in our friendship with God.

→ Do you ever catch yourself being God's phone-a-friend?

→ Have you ever been fickle about your relationship with God?

→ How can you become a better friend to God?

Prayer for Personal Revival

Lord, it is truly incredible that You call me friend.

What a privilege! You are the perfect Friend. There is nothing I want

more than to reciprocate. I don't want to be Your friend in name only,

but also in my actions and attitudes. Draw me close to Your side.

Help me cultivate an intimate friendship with You.

I want to be loyal, transparent, and selfless in our relationship.

Forgive me for the times my friendship toward You has been

one-sided, casual, or surface. Lord, I know that personal revival

is birthed out of intimacy with You, therefore make me thirsty

for a true, genuine, authentic friendship with You.

I love You, Lord! In Jesus' name I pray.

Amen.

DAY 27

Thirsty for the Cross

JAMES 4:4

LOOK BACK: Yesterday you committed to being an intimate friend to God. Talk to Him like He is the perfect friend. (He is!) As your day progresses, let loyalty, transparency, and selflessness toward God be seen in all your attitudes and actions.

The cross before me, the world behind me;
The cross before me, the world behind me;
The cross before me, the world behind me;
No turning back, no turning back.

The lyrics of this old hymn should be the anthem of every follower of Christ. The cross is the family crest of the household of faith. We live and move and have our being when we take shelter in its shade. If we took all the themes of Christianity and condensed them into one thematic centerpiece, it would be this: the cross.

No greater power exists than the message of the cross. The truth of Christ crucified is mightier than a supersonic jet, the world's fastest computer, and nuclear weaponry combined. The cross saves, heals, and sets the captives free. It is the only force on the face of the earth that can change the heart.

The cross of Christ Jesus is the bridge from death to life, foolishness to wisdom, and despondency to hope. It provides the passageway from lies to truth, fear to faith, and strongholds to freedom. Only the cross can change hate into love, weakness into strength, and sorrow into joy. Jesus' death on the cross gives us forgiveness of sins and the power not to sin.

Without the cross, we wouldn't be born again, possess a generation-shaking testimony, or have mountain-moving faith. Lost and confused, we would try to find the Way, Truth, and Life, but still be frantically searching. Without the cross we would be bound for hell.

I first knelt at the foot of the cross on December 26, 1989.

> *Lord, I ask You to take this messed-up girl. And if You can do anything with her life, I ask You to do it. I'll go wherever You ask me to go, do whatever You ask me to do, and say whatever You ask me to say. I'm Yours.*

This was my prayer when I became a follower of Christ. I had come to the end of myself. I was a raging alcoholic, filled with fear and depression, and heavy laden with sin. I was in desperate need of a Savior.

In that moment, Jesus revealed Himself to me as Lord and Savior. After giving my life to Jesus, I stood to my feet. The chains of alcohol addiction, fear, depression, and sin miraculously shattered. My life was forever changed. Freedom has a name. His name is Jesus.

And I've been kneeling at the foot of the cross ever since.

The struggle, however, is not to allow the world to distract us from the cross. Honestly, there is a continuous war for our affections and desires. The enemy of our souls would like nothing better than to sidetrack our attention toward anything else but the cross. Satan's nightmare is that our eyes are permanently affixed, without deviation, on the cross. So he uses the things of this world to entice us away.

What is "the world"? The world can take a myriad of anti-God forms, but includes philosophies, values, entertainment, behaviors, and imaginations that rebel against God. The system of this world stands diametrically opposed to the Kingdom of God.

The world is an enemy of the cross.

"You adulterers! Don't you realize that friendship with the world makes you an enemy of God? I say it again: If you want to be a friend of the world, you make yourself an enemy of God" (James 4:4). No one can serve the Lord without first renouncing their allegiance to the world. If we don't, we commit spiritual adultery and become an enemy of God.

To embrace the cross, we must shun the world. If we're devoted to the world, we've rejected the cross. It's that simple. There's no room for compromise.

Please get something settled in your heart and mind:

The world has absolutely nothing to offer.

Therefore, in every matter of life, we must continuously return to the cross. This is the good fight of faith in which all believers must engage.

- *Argument with your spouse?* See who can race faster to the foot of the cross.

- *Feeling hopeless?* Anchor yourself to the base of the cross.

- *Division or discord in your church?* Stand together and unified at the cross.

- *Loving your enemy seem difficult?* Receive God's unconditional love at the cross.

- *University student?* Scrutinize every philosophy through the filter of the cross.

- *Societal ills?* The cross is the answer.

- *Carrying too heavy of a load?* Place your burdens at the cross.

- *New wind of doctrine?* Use the cross as your measuring rod.

- *Doubts? Fears? Condemnation?* Run to the place where Jesus bore them—on the cross.

- *Christian walk off-kilter?* Regain your footing at the cross.

- *Dirty from sin?* Let God's rain of mercy wash you clean at the foot of the cross.

Revived Christians live at the cross, make much of the cross, and return quickly to the cross when they've drifted.

No turning back, no turning back.

Questions
for
Reflection

→ What surprised you the most from today's reading?

→ What areas of your Christian walk are enticed by the world?

→ Read and meditate on James 4:4. What is God speaking to you?

Prayer for Personal Revival

Lord, make me passionate about the cross.

I extricate myself from the things of this world.

Forgive me for the times I've committed spiritual adultery—

one foot at the cross and the other in the world.

I repent for divided affection and double-mindedness.

Help me make much of the cross and never return to the world.

Lord, give me a deep revelation that the world has nothing to offer except

heartache and misery. Jesus, I'm so grateful for Your death,

burial, resurrection, and ascension. Thank You for paying the price

of my salvation with Your blood, which dripped from the cross.

I love You, Lord! In Jesus' name I pray.

Amen.

DAY 28

Thirsty for Personal Retreats

1 KINGS 19

> **LOOK BACK:** Yesterday God revived your passion for the cross. Today, run every decision, problem, and idea through the filter of the cross. Any value system, entertainment, or philosophy that rebels against God is of the world. Determine to put all worldliness behind you—no turning back.

There have been seasons of my Christian walk when weariness engulfed me. Battle fatigued, I couldn't find the strength or resilience to continue. I was desperate to refuel, refocus, and reflect. I was desperate for rest.

Consider human-just-like-us Elijah. In 1 Kings 18, mighty Elijah possessed the spiritual strength to confront the prophets of Baal on Mount Carmel, and had the God-given ability to run faster than a horse. And just one chapter later, the wheels fell off Elijah's new Cadillac Escalade. This same (mighty?) Elijah fled in fear from Jezebel, and prayed he would die because it all got to be too much.

Just like our friend Elijah, you and I need to spend time alone with God, beneath a solitary broom tree (or house plant) of God's presence to renew our strength. While our daily time with the Lord is indispensable to our spiritual well being (nothing replaces it), I've found this to be true as well:

Recovery from a protracted battle often calls
for protracted time set apart with God.

Take center stage—drum roll please—*the personal prayer retreat.*

On a personal prayer retreat, you make time and space to give God your full attention. You spend unhurried time in His presence. You pursue God for, *well*—God. You lay your heart on His altar, renew your love affair with Him, and receive oxygen for your soul.

During a retreat, your soul stands alone with God. You unlearn and re-learn. God takes out, puts in, and rearranges. Your priorities get reshuffled. (It's amazing how God pinpoints the things that really matter—and don't.)

As you marinate in His presence and stop "doing" for God (He can raise up a donkey to do the same), you're reminded that the greatest yearning of your heart is this: "God, I desire You and You alone" (something a donkey can't do—worship God).

"But you don't know my calendar," you say. "I can't afford the time to take a personal prayer retreat." You can't afford *not* to. You may have to juggle or adjust, but it's there, somewhere. You just have to find it. Let me rephrase it like this: if we can find time to binge watch all nine seasons of _____, we can find extended time to *be with Jesus*. Please schedule it. Posthaste.

I've taken half-day, full-day, 24-hour, three-day, and seven-day retreats. My experience is this: if you don't have D-A-Y-S on end for a personal prayer retreat, God will honor the time you *can* dedicate to Him. But if you *can* steal away for an extended length of time, *do it!*

"Where can I go on retreat with the Lord?" Let me answer your question with a question:

Where do you best hear from God?

Our relationships with God are all so different. For me, God's voice is the loudest and His presence is most tangibly felt when I'm away from the familiar—literally anywhere, as long as it's unfamiliar. Elijah's place of refueling was a solitary broom tree. Where's yours?

I've taken prayer retreats holed up in a hotel room, a bed and breakfast, and in my church's prayer room. I've also spent prolonged time with God at a friend's home, as well as on a park bench staring at a lake (a half-day retreat location). Regardless of where your retreat is conducted—local or distant, expensive or frugal—it'll be a sacred space to meet with God.

At the start of my retreat, I anoint myself with oil to consecrate myself to God's purposes during my time with Him. Then I prayerfully determine the type of fast I'm going to undertake. Lastly, I pack my Bible, notebook and pen, worship music, and communion elements.

I also establish a loose retreat plan; "loose" because the Holy Spirit orchestrates the retreat and moves as He wills. But without even a relaxed structure, precious time is wasted as runaway thoughts can dictate the course of your retreat experience.

To help you get started, here is a sample retreat schedule that has proven highly effective for me:

- read Bible
- pray
- listen in silence
- journal
- give thanks
- worship
- rest.

Rinse and repeat this rhythm for the duration of the retreat.

Regardless of the retreat length, location, or schedule, accept Jesus' irresistible, personal-to-you invitation:

> "Come to Me, all you who labor and are heavily burdened, and I will give you rest. Take My yoke upon you, and learn from Me. For I am meek and lowly in heart, and you will find rest for your souls. For My yoke is easy, and My burden is light" (Matt. 11:28–30, MEV).

Jesus. Is. Your. Rest.

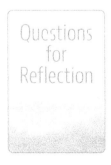

Questions for Reflection

→ What part of Elijah's story can you relate to?

→ Where do you best hear from God to refuel?

→ How can a prayer retreat help ignite personal revival?

Prayer for Personal Revival

Lord, I can't go on like this.

I'm exhausted and discouraged.

I've come to find refuge for my weary soul.

The battle has been long fought.

I lay my heart upon Your altar.

Lord, reach Your healing hand into my heart

and perform spiritual heart surgery.

I have bruises on top of bruises.

Close open wounds, soften scar tissue, and tear down walls.

I surrender my pain and disappointments to You.

Impart to me Your healing, strength, and love.

Oh, breath of God, revive me.

I love You, Lord! In Jesus' name I pray.

Amen.

DAY 29

Thirsty for Extraordinary Faith

HEBREWS 11

> **LOOK BACK:** Yesterday you learned about the correlation between retreats and revival. Today, if you haven't checked your calendar, take a step of faith and block out time for a personal prayer retreat. Whether your retreat is an afternoon or several days, expect God to breathe life into your weary soul.

I hate regrets!

I mean I *really* hate regrets. Oh, I have them. We all do. I have a slew. But I endeavor to live my life so I'll have as few as possible.

I do this so that when I get to the end of my life and am face-to-face with my Savior, I'll know that the entirety of my life counted for Him. I don't want to stand before Him, downcast, emptying my pockets of one regret after the next.

But want to know what I would regret the most? The regret of all regrets? Here it is: *that I didn't believe God more.* This translates to not trusting Him enough, not taking Him at His Word, not having faith that what He has promised will come to pass, and not asking God for more or bigger in prayer—especially with regard to the Kingdom.

There, I said it.

See, here's the thing: the longer we're in relationship with God, the greater measure of faith we should walk. The more we know Him, the higher our level of trust. The deeper our intimacy with Him, the bigger and bolder our prayers should be (small prayers are an insult to our big God). The bottom line is this:

We should have extraordinary faith in our extraordinary God.

But why is it such a struggle? Why don't we possess the extraordinary trust of the people listed in Hebrews 11—the Hall of Faith? They had abiding faith despite severe hardships or length of time a promise was made. They had unshakable faith no matter the difficulty of trial or intensity of persecution. They didn't throw away their confident trust, even at the point of death.

Oh, I'm sure they had their moments. We all do. But they didn't allow themselves to stay there. They picked themselves up by their spiritual bootstraps, shook off despondency and despair, and raised their faith shields high once again. Faith isn't faith until it is tested.

So how do we walk by extraordinary faith in our extraordinary God? Let me answer this question with a question. What is the opposite of walking by faith? Fear, doubt, unbelief? While none of these answers are wrong, there is a much clearer response that was right there all the time.

The opposite of walking by faith is walking by sight.

The apostle Paul says it this way, "For we live by believing and not by seeing" (2 Cor. 5:7). Christians who have extraordinary faith don't place their eyes on the external. Their confident trust is solely in Jesus. They keep their eyes on Him and His Word, no matter what's going on around them. This is the good fight of faith—keeping our eyes on Jesus.

And as we keep our eyes on God, we intentionally magnify His enormity over our problems. God is B-I-G. He is bigger than the worst circumstances we might endure. Nothing is impossible with Him. One touch from God's hand will untangle the tightest, most complicated knot.

Do you know how big God's hand is? Isaiah 40:12 provides the answer: "Who else has held the oceans in his hand? Who has measured off the heavens with his fingers?" The span of God's hand (your hand's span is from the tip of your pinky finger to the tip of your thumb) measures the waters of the earth. God literally measures the Atlantic, Pacific, Indian, and Arctic Oceans with just His hand!

If that's how big God's hand is, can you imagine how *huge* He must be? As we magnify the enormity of God over our problems, we'll have no problem believing He will do all He has promised. Extraordinary faith expects God to do the extraordinary.

So, practically speaking, what does extraordinary faith look like?

- You trust God for your prodigal child's salvation. But in addition, extraordinary faith believes God will use him or her to win multitudes for the Kingdom.

- You believe God will provide for your financial needs every month. But in addition, extraordinary faith believes God will give you a debt-reduction plan so you can generously give to the Kingdom.

- You pray for your personal needs to be met (which is biblical). But in addition, extraordinary faith asks God for the salvation of entire nations.

We live in dark times. The greatest need for Christians is to believe that God is who He says He is, and will do what He says He will do. While the world walks by extraordinary fear, God is calling His people to walk by extraordinary faith.

Often in the darkest of dark times, God divinely raises up His chosen instruments who will believe Him when others fall away. I want to be counted among those who trusted God in the most trying of circumstances. If there is a Hall of Faith in heaven, I don't want there to be an empty spot where my picture was supposed to hang. No, I want my portrait to be among the greats listed in Hebrews 11—the people who walked by extraordinary faith.

There is nothing you or I possess that is more valuable than our faith in Christ. *Nothing.*

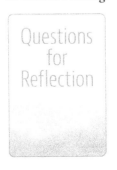

Questions for Reflection

→ Do you struggle with "walking by sight"?

→ Describe your view of God. Be honest— small or big?

→ Using a present trial in your life, explain how you can walk by extraordinary faith.

Prayer for Personal Revival

Lord, I want to walk by extraordinary faith.

Give me new spiritual lenses to view You

as enormous, and my problems as small.

Help me fix my gaze on You and not the situations in my life.

You've placed me on earth for such a time as this.

The kind of faith required in this hour is extraordinary.

Use me to show the rest of the world

how to trust You when so many don't.

I realize that as I fight the good fight of faith,

I'll impart courage to others around me.

I love You, Lord! In Jesus' name I pray.

Amen.

DAY 30

Thirsty for Jesus to Return

REVELATION 22:7-21

> **LOOK BACK:** Yesterday your extraordinary faith in Christ was awakened. Today, ask the Lord to help you keep your eyes off your circumstances, and instead onto Jesus and His Word. Walking by extraordinary faith will prepare you for the return of Christ.

The wedding guests stood to their feet as the double doors swung open and the cellist played the processional. Some craned their necks with eager anticipation, while others impatiently tapped their feet. However, all were aghast as they caught a glimpse of the bride starting down the aisle. She appeared to be dying.

The bride's wavy hair hung matted. She had dark circles, pale skin, and sunken cheekbones. Her bridal gown was soiled and torn. Every few steps, she held on to the end of a pew to catch her breath. However, the worst part of this horrifying scene was the reaction of the groom. Overcome by intense grief, he sobbed uncontrollably.

This morose portrait illustrates the Bride of Christ in the twenty-first century and the anguish of Almighty God over the spiritual condition of His people. The Church is in desperate need of revival. Personal revival remains the only hope for Christians who are lukewarm, worldly, and powerless.

Jesus, the Bridegroom, is coming! Are you ready?

All of history hangs on two golden hooks: the first coming of the Lord and the second coming of the Lord. We live in a transitional time between these greatest of all events. Jesus' birth is behind us; His return is ahead.

The last prayer in the Bible is found at the end of the last chapter: "Come, Lord Jesus!" (Rev. 22:20). Jesus revealed to John the apostle, on the Island of Patmos, the timeline of end-time events, including His return. John responds, "Come, Lord Jesus!" This three-word prayer should be the heart cry of every believer.

Have you ever missed someone so deeply you couldn't wait to see that person again—to the point you were lovesick? Our hearts should ache for Jesus' second coming in that same manner. However, much of the Church lives largely detached from His return. Although we proclaim our love for Jesus, we live satisfied with our earthly existence; the daily grind is our focus.

As we continue to live in the period between the two golden hooks, our desires and affections need to intentionally shift. We must transition our passion from the things of this world to a holy thirst for the return of our Bridegroom King. If we don't, we'll continue apathetic living regarding Christ's return.

Personal revival is the best preparation for the return of Christ. A fully revived Christian not only lives in a state of watchfulness for the coming of the Lord, but also provokes others to do the same. By virtue of their fiery love, believers who've experienced personal revival will expose and challenge lukewarm, indifferent, and non-committed Christians to become passionate about Jesus and His return.

While there is a plethora of metaphors used in Scripture to describe the Church (Body of Christ, Army of God, Family of God, Temple of God, etc.), it is the imagery of the Bride of Christ that most vividly portrays Christ the Bridegroom's relationship with His Church. The bridal paradigm in the Bible describes Jesus' intense, wholehearted love for His people.

The entirety of Scripture reveals the Bridegroom's affections, emotions, delights, and commitments to His Bride. No better imagery could convey His love for us, our eager expectation for His return, and the process of being made ready. I'm convinced that in order for our hearts to burn for the second coming of Christ, we need to possess a bridal identity. If we do, we'll live in a state of readiness, waiting in anticipation for the Day.

Here are some suggestions to see yourself as the Bride of Christ:

- See every aspect of the Kingdom of God through the eyes
  of a bride.

- Spend most of your time on wedding preparations.
- Love your Bridegroom with all of your heart, soul, mind, and strength.
- Have dove eyes for your Bridegroom only—never for another.
- Sit at your Bridegroom's feet in the bridal chamber of devotions.
- Sing love songs to your Bridegroom.
- Read and meditate on your Bridegroom's love letters to you.
- Daily ask your Bridegroom to return to you: "Come, Lord Jesus!"
- Share the intimate things of your heart with your Bridegroom.
- Wake up every morning, watching expectantly for your Bridegroom to return.
- Relish all the gifts your Bridegroom has bestowed upon you.
- Don't let distractions lull you to sleep and miss your Bridegroom's return.
- Don't allow scoffers to convince you that your Bridegroom isn't returning.
- Stay pure and unblemished for your Bridegroom.
- Remind others in the bridal company to prepare for the Bridegroom's return.
- Never forget the price your Bridegroom paid for you—His blood.
- Stay faithful to your Bridegroom, no matter what.

Picture a bride dressed in sparkling white, zealously in love with her Bridegroom. Her burning heart beats wildly with every thought of Him She loves Him, not for what He can do for her, but simply *for Him*. She has kept herself pure and chaste, without blemish or wrinkle. Her dove eyes remain fixed solely on Him; the world has completely lost its appeal.

Now imagine that bride running passionately down the aisle, full of life, to meet her Bridegroom. Revived, the Bride of Christ is now ready for Christ's return.

Lord Jesus, send revival, and let it begin with me!

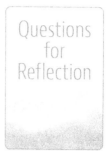
Questions
for
Reflection

→ Do you see "bride" as your primary identity in Christ?

→ Do you live like Jesus could return at any moment?

→ What changes must you make to ready yourself for Christ's return?

Prayer for Personal Revival

Lord, I want to view You as my Bridegroom.

Help me see every aspect of the Kingdom

through the eyes of a lovesick bride.

I want to long for Your return. Forgive me for focusing my attention

on the things of this world rather than on the Day You are returning.

I know that personal revival is the best preparation for Your second coming.

Revive any areas of my life that I'm not ready for Your return.

Let me be found faithful, pure, and unblemished.

Lord, give me dove eyes that are singly fixed on You.

Use me to prepare the Church, and the spiritually lost, for Your return.

I love you, Lord! In Jesus' name I pray.

Amen.

DAY 31

Thirsty for the Fire of the Holy Spirit

ACTS 2:1–21

> **LOOK BACK:** Yesterday, God renewed your thirst for His second coming. You now eagerly await the soon return of your Bridegroom. Today marks the end of our 31-day journey to personal revival with the last, but perhaps most important, element to personal revival—*fire*.

The Holy Spirit isn't the introverted, silent partner of the Trinity as some presume. He is the most powerful force this earth has ever seen. He is God.

The Holy Spirit is the fire of God. He doesn't have *some* fire. He *is* fire. His very presence is fire. And His fire isn't just symbolic, like the orange flame on the logo of many Christian denominations. He is the All-Consuming Fire.

The fire of the Holy Spirit is God's power, passion, and purity.

His fire leads, guides, and directs. His fire softens hearts. His fire changes the temperature of the cold and lukewarm to red-hot. His fire lights the darkness. His fire consumes sin. His fire spreads through Christian "brushfires" who start fires wherever they go.

The revival in Jerusalem on the Day of Pentecost (Acts 2) is a portrait of God's people experiencing personal revival. The 120 believers in the Upper Room were saturated with God. The fire that descended wasn't just a little candlewick upon their heads. It was the power of God burning within them to win the world for Jesus Christ. In turn, they carried that burning fire to the nations.

The essence of true scriptural Christianity is doing the works of Jesus empowered by the fire of the Holy Spirit. The fire of God provides the indispensable power needed for effective witnessing. The Book of Acts is the plumb line for Spirit-empowered Christian living; when it stops being the example, it becomes man-empowered ministry. Christians who are filled with the fire of the Holy Spirit are walking revivals.

Fire is identifiable. It's difficult to conceal. You don't have to advertise a fire. When there is a house fire, the local news station just shows up. People come from out of nowhere to watch it burn. They'll even stare at the aftermath of a fire—the ash and shell of the building. The fire of God is much more recognizable.

The people in Jerusalem were amazed as they saw the 120 saturated with the fire of the Holy Spirit. They asked, "How can this be? What can this mean? They're just drunk, that's all" (Acts 2:7, 12-13).

When you are consumed with the fire of the Holy Spirit, people will look at you and see the priorities of God, the activity of God, the power of God, and the love of God. They'll see Jesus in you.

The Holy Spirit moved with intense might in the Upper Room. He still does today. He is active and living and speaks. He enables natural humans to do supernatural exploits in order to fulfill the Great Commission.

I had an Upper Room experience that changed my life forever.

I had been frequenting a Christian bookstore in my local town. Each time I shopped in the store, I would strike up a conversation with the owner. Almost every time, she would talk to me about the fire of God. Honestly, I didn't pay much attention to what she was telling me, but she was relentless. She encouraged me to read the Book of Acts with fresh eyes.

One particular day, after yet another conversation with the bookstore proprietor, I went home and began reading Acts. When I got to Acts 2, a desperation for *more* of God came over me. I fell to my knees praying, "Lord, I want everything You have for me!"

I stood on my feet and worshiped God. As I did, a light and heat, like I had never before experienced, flooded that upstairs bedroom of our small Cape Cod-style house. It was like someone turned on a stadium lamp that shone through my bedroom window. With tears streaming down my face, all I could do was proclaim my love for Jesus.

My Christian walk has never been the same. That encounter with God changed my life forever. It felt like my spiritual engine was now operating on all eight cylinders instead of just two. After this encounter, I prayed with fire, praised with fire, and won souls with fire. I burned for Jesus. I was revived!

The impact that the fire of the Holy Spirit had on my life was immeasurable. Boy, was that Christian bookstore owner right! I needed the fire of God! We all do.

It's the responsibility of every child of God to get on fire for God. But you've got to want it. You can't embrace entertainment over fire. Comfort over fire. Dullness over fire. Status quo over fire. Man's opinion over fire. Anything over fire.

Don't be like the 380 who witnessed Jesus' resurrection, but didn't show up to the Upper Room as He instructed. Instead, imitate the 120 who obeyed Jesus and waited in the Upper Room for the fire of God to fall on them.

But here's another attribute of fire. Fire can go out. Just because you were on fire for God at one time, doesn't mean you are now. If that's you, cry out to God for His fresh fire!

Honestly, there is no time to waste. There is an urgency of the hour. These are the Last Days. We've got to stay sharp. We've got to stay keen. We've got to stay boiling hot for God. The salvation of souls depends upon it. The ability to hear direction from God, moment-by-moment in these turbulent times, depends upon it.

The fire of God is still available today. It's the same fire that the early Christians experienced in the Upper Room in Jerusalem. It's the same fire that filled me in the upstairs bedroom of my house in New Jersey 30 years ago. It isn't another fire. It's that same fire.

Ask the Holy Spirit to fill you with His fire. He will. He's been waiting for you to ask Him.

Questions for Reflection

→ Read Acts 2:1–21 through fresh eyes. What is God speaking?

→ How would you describe a Christian who is on fire for God?

→ Have you been longing for *more*?

Prayer for Personal Revival

Lord, thank You for the 31 days of this journey to personal revival.

I need Your fire. I want to burn for You.

All-Consuming Fire, let Your fire fall upon me.

I ask You to fill me to overflowing.

Saturate me with the fire of the Holy Spirit.

I want to be on fire for You in every area of my life.

Keep Your fire burning inside me.

Convict me if I'm ever tempted to let Your fire go out.

I receive Your fire now by faith.

From this day forward, I'm empowered to be Your witness.

I'll set the world ablaze with the gospel of Jesus Christ everywhere I go.

I love You, Lord! In Jesus' name I pray.

Amen.

Epilogue

Your *Thirsty* journey doesn't have to end here.

- If you incorporated this devotional into your morning devotions, start again and read a chapter before bed each night.

- Take a personal retreat utilizing the "Prayers for Personal Revival" that appear at the end of each day's reading.

- This time around, gather friends and family to take the journey with you.

- Dig deeper into the Scripture passages referenced for greater revelation.

- Prayerfully review the sections you underlined or starred. These are probably areas God highlighted to you.

- If you are slack in a particular area of your Christian walk, find that topic in *Thirsty's* Table of Contents. Ask God to revive that specific area of your relationship with Him.

- Purpose to take this 31-day journey yearly, every January (or whenever you feel the need) to stay revived.

- After you've read *Thirsty* inside out, over and over, keep it at your ready reference on your bookshelf.

Friend, now that you've experienced personal revival, go set the world ablaze with the gospel of Jesus Christ!

About the Author

Dr. Jamie Morgan is mantled to evangelize the nations, call the Church back to the place of prayer, fan the flame of revival, and mentor trailblazer leaders to do the same. She is a pastor, prayer warrior, writer, and revivalist.

Jamie is a member of America's National Prayer Committee and the Assemblies of God Prayer Committee. She holds an M.A. in Practical Theology from Oral Roberts University and a Doctor of Ministry from the Assemblies of God Theological Seminary.

Her weekly podcast, "Fire Starter with Dr. Jamie Morgan," on the Charisma Podcast Network, is designed to create a desperation for revival in the hearts of God's people. You can find her podcast on iTunes or anywhere podcasts are heard.

Jamie is the author of *A Journey to Ministry: Discover Your Calling, Purpose, and Destiny.* This book is her journey to ministry and illustrates how God will blast through any obstacle that gets in the way of answering God's call on your life. Allow her story to inspire you to step out in faith to do whatever God leads. Jamie has also been published in *Charisma News, Prayer Connect, The Christian Post, Fox News,* and other publications around the world.

But Jamie's most important role is wife, mother, mother-in-law, and grandmother. Her website is JamieMorgan.com.

A podcast to create a desperation for revival.

FIRE STARTER
with Dr. Jamie Morgan

CPN

Features interviews with revivalists, field reports on present-day moves of God, and teachings on revival.

Join the Fire Starter family of revivalists.

Listen on iTunes and everywhere podcasts are heard.

Prayer Ascending
Revival Burning
Laborers Evangelizing
Nations Awakening

JAMIE MORGAN
— MINISTRIES —

JAMIEMORGAN.com

If you enjoyed *Thirsty*, your friends might be thirsty, too!

Multiple copy discounts of *Thirsty* are available at prayershop.org

*Prayer*CONNECT

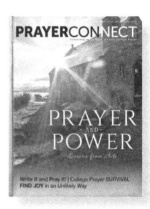

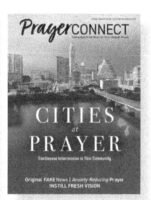

A QUARTERLY MAGAZINE DESIGNED TO:

Mobilize believers to pray God's purposes for their church, city and nation.

Connect intercessors with the growing worldwide prayer movement.

Equip prayer leaders and pastors with tools to disciple their congregations.

Each issue of *Prayer Connect* includes:
- Practical articles to equip and inspire your prayer life.
- Helpful prayer tips and proven ideas.
- News of prayer movements around the world.
- Theme articles exploring important prayer topics.
- Connections to prayer resources available online.

Print subscription: $24.99
(includes digital version)

Digital subscription: $19.99

Church Prayer Leaders Network membership: $35.99 (includes print, digital, and CPLN membership benefits)